The Celluloid Literature

The Celluloid Literature

film in the humanities

Second Edition

William Jinks

University of Florida, Gainesville

GLENCOE PRESS
A division of Benziger Bruce & Glencoe, Inc.
Beverly Hills
Collier Macmillan Publishers
London

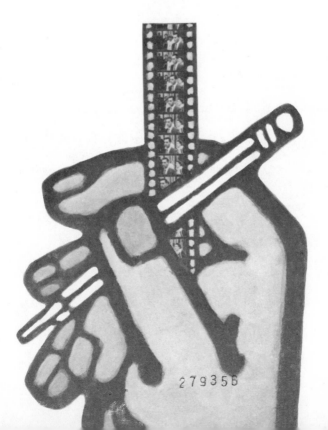

279356

PN
1994
J5
1974

Glencoe Press
A division of Benziger Bruce & Glencoe, Inc.
8701 Wilshire Boulevard
Beverly Hills, California 90211
Collier-Macmillan Canada, Ltd.

Library of Congress catalog card number: 73-7361

First printing, 1974

To Sandy

Contents

Acknowledgments

Acknowledgment is gratefully made to the following publishers who have generously granted permission to use selections from their publications:

Harcourt Brace Jovanovich, Inc., for: "The Organic Structure of *Potemkin*" by Sergei Eisenstein, from *Film Form: Essays in Film Theory* by Sergei Eisenstein, edited and translated by Jay Leyda, copyright, 1949, by Harcourt Brace Jovanovich, Inc. and reprinted with their permission.

Macmillan Publishing Co., Inc., for: "The Course of Italian Neo-Realism" by Arthur Knight. Reprinted with permission of Macmillan Publishing Co., Inc. from *The Liveliest Art* by Arthur Knight. © Arthur Knight 1957.

University of California Press, for: "Citizen Kane and Citizen Hearst" by Charles Higham, from *The Films of Orson Welles* by Charles Higham, University of California Press, 1970. Originally published by the University of California Press; reprinted by permission of The Regents of the University of California.

Preface to the Second Edition

THE ORIGINAL edition of *The Celluloid Literature* was inspired, in part, by the notion that the narrative film and literature in general (the novel in particular) shared a great many features. The two years since that edition appeared have served to confirm this impression. Interviews with film directors, for instance, reveal that by and large they are highly literate individuals, who actively seek cinematic equivalents for what are essentially literary techniques. And, of course, the reverse is also true: novelists and playwrights have continued to adapt freely from contemporary film narratives.

Thus, the changes in this new edition have been restricted to a few key areas. In chapter 1, a general comparison of film and literature has been substituted for the detailed analogy between the rise of the novel and the development of early film. The glossary and bibliography have been considerably expanded to include recent terms and materials, and the list of film distributors has been updated. Chapter 6, on film criticism, is entirely new.

In this new chapter, care is taken to distinguish between the concerns of reviewer, critic, scholar, and theorist. The various ways these writers might approach a film—in terms of social comment, abstract ideas, director's background, artistic elements, and so on—are analyzed in much greater depth than in the first edition. And this discussion has been enlarged to incorporate two additional methods: the biographical approach and the genre study. The short essays that accompanied the original chapter have been replaced by three longer, more important pieces, which serve to illustrate some of the different approaches.

Any book of this kind obviously owes a lot to many individuals who have thought or written about the film. To express all indebtedness would be impossible, but for encouragement, advice, and critical guidance I would like to single out a few who have been particularly helpful: George Gath, who nurtured this book from the very outset to its completion; Tony Velie, whose advice and month-to-month encouragement were of inestimable value; Don Rea, for his careful, detailed criticism of the original manuscript; and lastly, René Wellek and Austin Warren, whose *Theory of Literature* provided the basis for the critical concepts outlined in chapter 6.

W.J.

Introduction

Arriving when it did on the very eve of the twentieth century, the film offered the storyteller an entirely new means of shaping a work of fiction. Like the novel, an older narrative predecessor, film soon learned to incorporate and absorb what it needed from other arts. Music, for example, provided a model for rhythm and counterpoint and theater an understanding of the nature of spectacle. It is the literary form, however, with which film has always shared the greatest number of affinities.

Superficially, film appears to resemble a kind of "canned theater." But while its means of representation is visual, its method of artistic control is actually very close to that of the novel. For example, a film maker, like a novelist, can instantly shift our attention from a vast panorama to the most minute detail because, in the film, our attention is not free to wander as it is in the theater. In addition, it is clear that the film maker, unlike the dramatist, is not confined to the physical limitations of the stage.

Film, of course, did indeed draw from the theater as it did from the novel, and since the narrative film was able to emulate and to learn from the older narrative arts, it attained artistic maturity in a short period of time. As French film critic André Bazin once suggested, "It may be that the past twenty years in the cinema will be reckoned in its overall history as the equivalent of five centuries in literature." From this standpoint, today's film emerges as a relatively mature art form.

It is difficult, for example, to ignore the fact that many of the outstanding narratives of the twentieth century have been films. Film makers such as Chaplin, Eisenstein, Renoir, Welles, Bresson, Antonioni, Bergman, Fellini, and Resnais have bequeathed us a body of work whose significance is only now beginning to be understood. In addition to its own legacy, the film has had a direct influence on contemporary fiction as well. Its impact on the work of John Dos Passos, William Burroughs, and Alain Robbe-Grillet, to name only a few writers, has been fairly well established.

But, even more importantly, the filmed narrative has permanently altered the way in which we respond to fiction. Stylistic techniques that originated in film, such as the flashback, the dissolve, slow motion, and montage, have slowly found their way into the novel and the short story. Under the influence of film, the often ornate rhetoric of the eighteenth and nineteenth centuries has given way to the terse "realistic" dialogue of the twentieth century. In addition, the camera's singularly objective manner of narrating a story has given rise to a point of view that is often described as the "fly-on-the-wall" or "camera" point of view. Thus, the film has not only influenced the existing modes of fiction, but it has extended them by offering the storyteller an alternative means of narration—the film form itself.

Film and literature are, of course, two very different kinds of experience. However, in writing *The Celluloid Literature* I have elected to concentrate on those areas that are common to both literature and the narrative film. I want this book to accomplish two goals: first, to provide the reader with an introduction to the film art, and second, to emphasize how close, both in form and in content, literature and the narrative film are to one another.

It also seems to me that the simultaneous consideration of these two closely related forms can only enrich our understanding of both literature and film. The study of film can in no way diminish the important values of the more traditional literary genres; it can only serve to augment and perhaps even reinvigorate them. Film has the ability to reawaken us to the power of the sensuous image and the expressive richness of gesture and movement. In addition, it also seems clear to me that much of the methodology of literary analysis is equally applicable to the study of film. If we can simply learn to consider the film not as an isolated phenomenon of the twentieth century, but rather as a continuation of the traditional narrative arts, we will readily discover that it has managed to retain and keep viable all that has been central to the narrative tradition.

The Celluloid Literature

Fig. I-A
The house in this shot might be a sharecropper's cabin during the depression; on the other hand, it might epitomize a proud, historic survivor from our agricultural past. With only the single frame to work from, it is difficult to decide what a given picture represents. See page 2.

1

THE WORD
AND
THE IMAGE:

LANGUAGE

> In the novel, you start with a bag of words, and the way you put the words together has meaning. In the movies, you get another kind of vocabulary. You have little bits of film strips, each the equivalent of words —five words or five thousand. But the strips are put together as individual words. Constructing a movie out of the field of experience that you have recorded gets to be wholly fascinating because you are working with a brand new vocabulary. You are putting things together in a way that nobody has ever put them together before.

NORMAN MAILER[1]

One of the exciting features of the film experience is its immediacy—the fact that the film is occurring *right now*. Here, a group of Algerian nationalists attacks French soldiers in Gillo Pontecorvo's *Battle of Algiers* (1968).

Courtesy of Audio Film Center/Ideal Pictures

In Robert Enrico's "Occurrence at Owl Creek Bridge" (1961), the experiences of an entire day are compressed into a split-second.

The literal-mindedness of the camera tends to wed the character and the role forever. It is, for example, very difficult to imagine *The Graduate* without Dustin Hoffman.

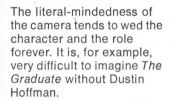

No ONE would argue that film and literature are the same medium or even the same kind of experience. The primary thrust of literature is linguistic, hence indirect; while the impetus of film is imagistic and immediate. And yet, despite the obvious differences separating these two narrative forms, there are some rather startling resemblances between them.

If the modern film is carefully considered, it becomes evident that it is heavily indebted to other, older art forms. For example, it draws freely upon the tradition of live theater, especially the techniques of staging, lighting, movement, and gesture; from the novel it borrows structure, characterization, theme, and point of view; from poetry, an understanding of metaphor, symbolism, and other literary tropes; from music, rhythm, repetition, and counterpoint; and from painting, a sensitivity to shape and form, visual textures, and color.

Though all these elements are closely interwoven in today's films, they were not much in evidence in the first movies. As Erwin Panofsky points out in his essay "Style and Medium in the Motion Pictures," these early films were produced to exploit a brand new technology,[2] not to satisfy a set of artistic criteria. And they were designed to fill the movie houses of major cities—theaters like Koster & Bial's in New York, the Cinéma Saint-Denis in Paris, and the Kino unter den Linden in Berlin. The audiences that flocked to this new form of entertainment were neither wealthy nor educated; they were composed almost exclusively of lower-middle-class workers and their families.

The sporadic development of the popular film, curiously enough, had much in common with the emergence of the eighteenth-century novel. Similarly, the initial audience for these moralistic adventure novels was primarily the urban middle class. As Martin S. Day suggests:

> The eighteenth century saw a vastly increased reading public, chiefly of the middle class. Practical and down to earth, this class wanted to read about people it could recognize from its own observations and described in the language it employed. It preferred its stories to end with financial and domestic rewards, its own clear-cut goals in life.[3]

Ian Watt, in *The Rise of the Novel*, contends that as a consequence of the novel's popularity, the middle classes became the center of gravity of the reading public.[4] Like the early movies, the novel was deemed strictly a popular entertainment; subsequently it developed into the significant genre it is today, "largely independent of traditional literary standards [and] unsanctified by established critical canons."[5]

But the parallels went even deeper than similarities of audience. Both the eighteenth-century novel and the turn-of-the-century film relied heavily upon realism as a technique. Furthermore, both showed an unprecedented concern with the daily lives of ordinary people. Thus, any individual was a potential subject for a novel or film. Kenneth Macgowan, in *Behind the Screen*, wrote that the first movie program he saw, in 1897, consisted of two short films: "The first showed a half-dozen men diving into a pool; the other, two girls who leaped out of bed to have a pillow fight that ended with feathers filling the air."[6]

Because of the subject matter they depicted and the audience they attracted, both the fledgling cinema and the early novels were held in low social repute. Panofsky notes that as late as 1905 there was only one movie house in Berlin, and that when the "better classes" ventured inside the theater, it was considered a kind of slumming.[7] And Ian Watt remarks that "The novel was widely regarded as a typical example of the debased kind of writing by which the booksellers pandered to the reading public."[8]

The novel, of course, soon became more acceptable, as men of extraordinary imagination and ability applied their talents to this new narrative form. Daniel Defoe, with *Robinson Crusoe* (1719) and *Moll Flanders* (1722), was one of the first major artists to experiment with the novel. And by 1750, both Samuel Richardson's *Pamela* and Henry Fielding's *Tom Jones* had been published and enjoyed by a wide audience. Throughout the nineteenth century, the novel form was developed and refined into a major medium of literary expression.

By contrast, the development of film techniques progressed at a much faster rate. The reason for this is fairly simple: early film makers were able to draw upon the techniques, conventions, and innovations of literature, specifically the novel. For instance, one of the many apocryphal stories concerning D. W. Griffith, a truly great film innovator, maintains that he always carried a

Charles Dickens novel with him when he was on location. Once, when questioned about his unique editing style, Griffith reportedly asked: "Doesn't Dickens write that way?"[9]

The technical, thematic, and stylistic similarities between Dickens and Griffith were discussed at length by the Russian director Sergei Eisenstein in an essay entitled "Dickens, Griffith, and the Film Today." Eisenstein himself, another great innovator, also drew heavily upon literary sources. For example, in his essay "The Organic Structure of Potemkin" (see pp. 176–179), he acknowledges that the structure of his own highly acclaimed *The Battleship Potemkin* (1925) was modeled after the five-act division of classical tragedy.

The parallels between the film and the novel are so numerous and persistent that Susan Sontag, in *Against Interpretation*, argues that the history of the cinema in a sense mirrors the history of the novel.

> The fifty years of the cinema present us with a scrambled recapitulation of the more than two hundred year history of the novel. In D. W. Griffith, the cinema had its Samuel Richardson; the director of *Birth of a Nation* (1915), *Intolerance* (1916), *Broken Blossoms* (1919), *Way Down East* (1920), *One Exciting Night* (1922), and hundreds of other films voiced many of the same moral conceptions and occupied an approximately similar position with respect to the development of the film art as the author of *Pamela* and *Clarissa* [Samuel Richardson] did with respect to the development of the novel.[10]

This, of course, is not to imply that every great director has his literary counterpart in a novelist, but simply to suggest that the film, in a highly accelerated manner, was able to utilize the techniques of narrative fiction.

Almost from the beginning, however, there has existed a close relationship between film and literature. John Huston, for instance, wrote short stories for *The American Mercury* before Samuel Goldwyn brought him to Hollywood in the early '30s. In fact, during the '40s and '50s, many well-known novelists were writing screenplays: James Agee (John Huston's *The African Queen* [1952]), Raymond Chandler (Billy Wilder's *Double Indemnity* [1944], Alfred Hitchcock's *Strangers on a Train* [1951]), William Faulkner (Howard Hawks' *To Have and Have Not*

[1944] and *The Big Sleep* [1946]), Graham Greene (Carol Reed's *The Third Man* [1949]), John O'Hara (Michael Curtiz' *The Best Things in Life Are Free* [1956]), Budd Schulberg (Elia Kazan's *On the Waterfront* [1954]), John Steinbeck (Elia Kazan's *Viva Zapata* [1952]). Playwrights, as well, were making their own contributions: Noel Coward (Noel Coward and David Lean's *In Which We Serve* [1942], David Lean's *Brief Encounter* [1945]), Moss Hart (George Cukor's *A Star is Born* [1955]), George S. Kaufman (who collaborated with Morrie Ryskind on Sam Wood's Marx Brothers' classic *A Night at the Opera* [1935]), Harold Pinter (Joseph Losey's *The Servant* [1963]), Gore Vidal and Tennessee Williams (Joseph Mankiewicz' *Suddenly Last Summer* [1959]). More recently, there appears to be a trend among novelists and playwrights to script and direct their own films: Norman Mailer (*Wild 90* [1968], *Beyond the Law* [1968]), Alain Robbe-Grillet (*The Man Who Lies* [1971]) and Susan Sontag (*Duet for Cannibals* [1969]). The interest of novelists and playwrights in the film form is readily understandable, since each form contends with similar aesthetic problems: plot, dramatization of ideas, and highly individualized character studies.

The similarities in origin, narrative devices, and subject matter of the early films and novels are perhaps predictable. What does come as a surprise, however, is the discovery that film maker and novelist attain meaning through similar patterns of organization.

What follows, then, is an extended analogy between the basic structural units of the novel—the word, sentence, paragraph, and chapter—and the elemental building blocks of the film—the frame, shot, scene, and sequence. And though Ezra Pound is very right in asserting that "you can *prove* nothing by analogy. [It] is either range-finding or fumble,"[11] the analogy can sometimes make the unfamiliar more accessible by relating it to the familiar. Thus, it is possible to recognize that—even though film is essentially a visual experience and literature a linguistic one—these two "languages" share a remarkable number of similarities.

In a study of the aesthetics of poetry, Ezra Pound devotes a portion of his *ABC of Reading* to a consideration of the Chinese ideogram. By examining the ideogram, Pound is able to point up economically and graphically an essential characteristic of poetry

—that the ideogram "means the thing or the action or situation, or quality . . . that it pictures":[12]

人   木   白   東 sun tangled in the tree's branches,
man   tree   sun   as at sunrise, meaning now the east

With a Chinese ideogram, the reader receives both the symbol (the ideogram itself) and the object represented (the suggestible image) simultaneously. No one would be apt to confuse the symbol (人) with the man it represents, and yet clearly it was designed to suggest the configuration of a man. The same is true of the film representation of a man. Who would confuse a close-up of a man's face (represented on the screen by a twenty-five-foot-tall image) with the actual man? Thus, every narrative must take the form of *mimesis*—that is, an imitation of nature; or move toward invention, the creation of an unprecedented depiction of reality; or a combination of the two. Hence, nothing can *be* the represented object except the object itself (a variation of Gertrude Stein's "Rose is a rose is a rose").

The word and the image are similar in that they are both visual phenomena—they must both be perceived with the eye. On one hand, the string of letters that make up *farmhouse* demands that the reader convert the lifeless and yet suggestive word into an approximation of what the author intended. Transposing a word to an internalized image will necessarily evoke a highly individualized response, because everyone's experience of a farmhouse differs. To a boy raised in a city slum, *farmhouse* might mean "health," "contentment," "peace"; to a country boy who left home, it might mean "chores," "boredom," "endless, mindless drudgery." In short, the word "farmhouse" will be interpreted by the reader for himself.

On the other hand, it would seem that the film maker is able to exert a greater degree of control over his medium than the writer, since the picture of a farmhouse is much more explicit than the word itself. That is, it is not necessary to *translate* a picture into a mental image—film is literal, concrete, and explicit. The film maker is able to show precisely the farmhouse he has in mind—he doesn't have to trust that the reader will "see" the same farmhouse.

Yet, because his medium is so explicit, the film maker cannot utilize the kinds of ambiguities inherent in language that enable the novelist to suggest more than he says. For example, a novelist might write: "The weathered red barn in back of the house somehow always gave me a comforting feeling of security whenever I looked at it." The film maker can present a barn that is visually attractive, solid in appearance, but he cannot depend on his viewer to perceive the barn as an emblem of security unless he is willing to have an off-camera voice blatantly announce: "Please view this barn as a symbol of security." Yet despite the different degrees of explicitness and connotative control, both artists must work with "languages" that function in a remarkably similar fashion.

For the writer, the most integral unit of creation is the *word*. It is from the word that he creates his sentences, paragraphs, chapters, and ultimately, his book. For the film maker, the basic building block is the *frame*—a single transparent picture on a strip of film. Isolated, both the word and the frame have meaning, but that meaning is imprecise—the word and frame must be set in a context to clarify their meaning.

The word "quiver," for example, could be a reference to either a case for holding arrows—in which instance it would be a noun—or it might describe a particular kind of action as a verb. Even if the reader is able to assume that what he is dealing with is a verb rather than a noun, the ambiguity is still unresolved, for the reader is still unclear as to the nature of the verb. The verb could be indicating the movement that an arrow describes when it comes to rest, or simply the nature of a motion like a shaking movement—a tremor. Even if the reader is further advised that the verb is not describing the motion of an arrow, he still isn't quite sure as to how to perceive the essential character of the quivering movement—the tremor. If this motion, for example, describes a leaf, it is one thing; if it describes, on the other hand, a girl, it is something else again, for the tremor could be simply a reaction to the cold, or perhaps even the reaction to a fright—there even exists the possibility that it might be a combination of both fear and inclement weather.

Again, it might appear that with film, no such problem would exist because of the explicitness of the frame—it provides far more information than the single ambiguous word. And yet notice what happens when a viewer is confronted with the single frame. In Figure I-A the viewer sees the image of a cabin. The cabin appears to be unpainted pine with a wood-shingled roof, and from the outside the cabin appears to be a single large room. A simple chimney runs up the side of the windowless cabin. The background appears to be bean fields. The image might represent a sharecropper's house during the early depression days; but even if it does, despite the viewer's assurance of *what* he is seeing, there is still some doubt as to *how* to see the cabin. With only the single frame from which to work, it is very difficult to decide in what kind of context the picture needs to be placed, because several possibilities exist.

Perhaps the viewer is supposed to perceive the house as a nostalgic memory of a less complicated, less anxiety-ridden past. In this case, the frame takes on the kind of hard and simple beauty that James Agee[13] captured so well in his *Let Us Now Praise Famous Men*.

The house may appear in a documentary concerning the conditions of poverty in the United States. In this instance, the house is not a remnant of the past, but an eyesore in the present. It is a testimony to the discrepancies that exist between the "Haves" and the "Have-nots." Here the viewer would see the "shack" in the house, would probably feel sympathy or sorrow, perhaps even indignation.

The house may also appear in another kind of documentary —one produced by a government bureau, concerning the history of farming in the United States. Now the cabin represents only a survival of the historic past—an artifact. In this instance, the house (no longer a shack, notice) may well evoke pleasure on the part of the viewer. In comparing the contemporary farm dwellings with the cabin, the viewer is even made to feel proud that the standard of living has been raised so substantially. Just as the reader would need to see "quiver" in the context of a sentence before he could be clear about the meaning of the word, the viewer would need to see the single frame of the farmhouse within the context of the shot.

A sentence typically clarifies the meaning of an individual word, sets it in a more meaningful perspective. In a complete sentence the word "quiver" would attain a more explicit meaning: *She quivered slightly at the coolness of the night air, then proceeded alone up the deserted street.* From this sentence, it is clear that the girl's quivering is the result of the night air, that the motion is a sign of physical discomfort. At the same time, the sentence is colored slightly by the phrase *then proceeded alone up the deserted street.* The additional information—that she is alone, that it is dark, quiet, and chilly—suggests a feeling of fear, of foreboding. Thus, in this sentence the word "quivered" seems to convey both physical discomfort and fear.

In order to provide the same degree of clarity for the film viewer, it would be necessary for him to see a *shot*—a fragment of a film which has been taken, either actually or apparently, in one uninterrupted running of the camera. The shot, in other words, serves the same function for the film maker that the sentence does for the novelist. For example, if a film maker were shooting an important tennis match and wanted to indicate the tension of the contest to an audience, it is very unlikely that he would follow the exchanges of the match like a spectator. That approach would not only be repetitive, monotonous, and dizzying to follow, but it would probably also be completely devoid of tension—the viewer would be so caught up in the very mechanics of watching that the excitement of the match would be lost. To evoke the feeling of tension inherent in the match, the film maker would probably cut extensively during the event. (A *cut* is an instantaneous transition from one shot to another and is usually easy to spot in a film because it is invariably accompanied by a shift of camera position.) He might open with a long shot of the two antagonists facing each other, then cut to a medium shot of the player who was serving, then perhaps to a close-up of the taut face of the player waiting to return the ball. In this instance, the slowing down and breaking up of the action—converting it into shots—has helped to convey the tension involved in the contest.

There is no "average" shot. A shot can be as brief as a single frame. Robert Breer's *Fist Fight* (1964), for example, uses a different shot for almost every frame in the film. On the other hand, the length of a shot is limited only by the amount of film that a cameraman, in one continuous or apparently continuous filming, can shoot. French director Jean-Luc Godard, in his film *Weekend* (1968), reputedly used a tracking shot of a young couple in an automobile that was three hundred meters long (nearly a thousand feet of film).[14]

For the viewer, then, a shot of the farmhouse discussed above is clearly easier to "read" than the single frame—like the sentence, the shot provides an enlarged context. For example, the viewer might first see the farmhouse at a distance of fifty feet or so, then perhaps the camera begins to zoom* in toward the house and stops only when the doorway of the house nearly fills the entire screen (both the establishing shot of the house and the succeeding zoom would be considered one shot). Perhaps the camera remains focused on the doorway for a moment, and soon a woman comes to the door carrying a bucket. She wears a torn, ill-fitting cotton dress, and though her body looks young, her face appears drawn and haggard, and her shoulders seem to bend forward slightly. She leans against the doorframe and, for a moment, looks rather vacantly in the direction of the horizon. There is something about her stance that suggests a "bone-tired" kind of weariness. The shot concludes with her standing in the doorway.

This single shot might be as short as ten seconds; yet notice how much information it conveys. First, it becomes apparent that the house and its occupant are not being romanticized—the stark, weary figure of the woman precludes that kind of an interpretation. Second, although it is not impossible, it is unlikely that the footage represents an excerpt from a documentary concerning this nation's farming history. There are clues within the shot itself that suggest what the film maker is doing. The establishing shot (a shot that sets the scene) seems to remain with the house only long enough to suggest location; then it quickly moves to the doorway of the house, implying that it is the occupant or occupants of the house who are the real focus of attention. Also, the woman in the doorway is presented in a very special way. There is the contradiction between her youthful body and prematurely aged face; there comes the realization that she carries the water to the door because she probably has no plumbing; there is pathos in the sudden knowledge that she continues to wear what is

---

*A zoom lens is a lens whose focal length can be changed, thus altering the magnification of the image.

clearly a rag because she has nothing to replace it with. These carefully selected details shape the response of the viewer just as surely as the phrase *then proceeded alone up the deserted street* alters and implements the verb *quiver*. Though the question of *what* the word or shot refers to is answered in part by the context, other questions in the reader's and viewer's minds remain to be solved. But expectations of answers have been raised, and these answers can be provided through referring to a broader context.

A paragraph, a series of closely related sentences, typically gives the reader additional information about a particular "key" sentence in it, as in the case of the sentence about the solitary girl:

> The car seemed to be in the throes of death, the way it jerked and stalled. She looked at the gas gauge and discovered the source of her problem—it read empty. She was in a section of town where even the residents stayed behind carefully locked doors at night, and her face showed apprehension as she let the car drift to the curb. After securing the car doors, she stepped out onto the sidewalk. She quivered slightly at the coolness of the night air, then proceeded alone up the deserted street.

This paragraph, it should be noted, is set up much as a film maker might conceive a five-shot scene—an interior close-up shot of the girl being jostled about in the car; an extreme close-up of a gas gauge reading empty, followed by a shot of her tense face; a medium shot of the car drifting toward the curb; a medium-close shot of the girl locking the car and walking up the street of the deserted neighborhood. In this instance, the paragraph has revealed how the girl came to be in this particular predicament, and the paragraph also confirms the implications of fear that previously were only suggested.

A *scene* is ordinarily an action which is unified around a specific action or event and, normally, is also united by considerations of a time and place. The following three-shot scene of the sharecropper's cabin would remove most of the aforementioned ambiguity as to the type of film the audience is seeing:

```
Shot #1: Medium shot of the cabin; a slow zoom shot
         stopping when the doorway of the cabin fills the
         frame. A woman, walking from the interior, appears
         in the doorway holding a pan of water. She looks
         toward the camera.
```

```
cut to:
Shot #2: Long shot of a man, perhaps a quarter of a mile
         away, walking along a dirt road that is lined
         sparsely with pines. His feet set up small, barely
         discernible puffs of dust as he walks.
cut to:
Shot #3: The woman, as she was before, looking toward the
         camera. Abruptly she tosses the water into the
         yard and returns to the darkened interior of
         the house.
```

With this scene, the viewer's speculations are, in part, resolved. No longer is it necessary for him to guess how he should "read" the information he is witnessing. The hardship, the weariness of the people's lives has become readily apparent. It is also apparent, from this three-shot scene, that the film maker is able to exert the kind of artistic control that is ordinarily associated only with the novelist.

In the case of a novelist, there are literally no limitations on what can be described; he can, in fact, set on paper whatever he is capable of imagining. The dramatist, however, has less freedom, for the form with which he works imposes certain restraints upon him. The dramatist cannot, for example, show the husband returning home—this would have to be eliminated or indicated by means of dialogue. In addition, the film maker's control of his material, like the novelist's, is more selective. The dramatist would not be able to forcibly bring our attention to bear on the woman standing in the doorway, as the film maker has done. Rather, he would have to "attract" his audience's attention by means of placement of actors and actresses, staging, dialogue, or perhaps the use of lighting. The same considerations, of course, would hold true for the girl stranded in the forbidding neighborhood. Unless he were willing to go to a great deal of trouble, the dramatist would not be able to stage that particular scene. Again, he would have to employ dialogue to relate this information to the audience. The film maker, however, could easily realize this scene.

Eventually the novelist combines his paragraphs into larger units—chapters. In many respects, the chapter resembles an expanded paragraph; it is usually unified by one central focus. A chapter could derive its unification from a single incident or event; it might cover the events of a particular period of time—an hour, day, year, or even a generation. A chapter could limit itself to a description of a single character. Sometimes unity can be achieved by means of a physical setting: a room, a town, or a country.

In the example of the stranded girl, the episode of her running out of gas might be just one of many similar unpleasant occurrences in the same chapter. Earlier, she may have been threatened over the telephone. Sometime later, an inexplicable fire takes place in the kitchen of her house while she is asleep. While crossing the street, she narrowly averts being run over by an automobile. Finally, she runs out of gas in a dangerous neighborhood. All of these incidents might have one thing in common: the deliberate terrorizing of the girl. Thus, the incidents form a common thread that unifies the chapter into a coherent whole.

Chapters, like paragraphs, are distinct divisions of a novel and are usually characterized by coherence, unity, and completeness. It is difficult, however, to say *exactly* what it is that distinguishes a paragraph from a chapter. Typically, the chapter is much longer than a paragraph, but there are instances of chapters in novels being no longer than a couple of sentences (Laurence Sterne's innovative *Tristram Shandy* and Ken Kesey's *One Flew Over the Cuckoo's Nest* are two obvious examples). The problem is even more complicated when the *sequence*—the film's equivalent of the chapter—is considered.

The film, for example, does not have its narrative neatly divided into chapters (although British film maker Lindsay Anderson, in a film entitled *If . . .* [1969], did utilize an eight-part chapter-like division). The sequence—a series of closely related scenes—is subject to precisely the same criteria as the chapter: namely, unity, coherence, and completeness. In some instances, such as Anderson's *If . . .*, or Stanley Kubrick's *2001: A Space Odyssey* (1969) with its three-part division, the separation between sequences is apparent. In most films, however, it is more difficult to recognize and define the divisions.

The previously described scene of the sharecroppers would, most likely, represent a part of a sequence. The entire film might be composed of three thirty-minute sequences. This scene would be part of the first sequence, depicting the poverty and deprivation of a single family in the rural South. This first sequence might conclude with the family's decision to move north to a large city, and hopefully, a better life. The second sequence might describe their journey to the North, while the third could reveal the protagonists in their new environment. As with chapters in a novel, the possibilities for creating sequences are virtually unlimited; the artist need merely establish the relationship of one scene to another.

In order to compare the language of film with the language of literature, it was necessary to ignore, for the most part, the very striking dissimilarities of the two genres. Although a metaphor and a simile can enlarge perception by comparing the familiar with the unfamiliar or by examining something in a slightly altered perspective, it is essential to consider the peculiarities of each of the genres in order to determine how they differ from each other.

To begin with, film is a multi-sensory communal experience emphasizing immediacy, whereas literature is a mono-sensory private experience that is more conducive to reflection. A film is usually viewed in the presence of others who necessarily become part of the total gestalt of the film experience. Ideally, each member of the audience respects the presence of others and opens himself to the film. A tall hat, a noisy popcorn chewer, or a self-appointed narrator can adversely affect the impact of the film. The responses of the audience can also affect the perception of a film—an inappropriate laugh can provoke irritation, while infectious laughter can increase delight.

A novel, however, is typically a private experience, in which the relationship between the author and the reader is relatively direct and immediate. The responses of others do not impinge on the novel as they do on the film. The novel is also conducive to reflection, as the reader can pause and consider an important passage or mull over a particular phrase. This convenience, of course, is denied the viewer because the film moves unceasingly toward its conclusion (though developments in cassette television may soon change this).

But the film and the novel are alike insofar as their order is typically linear. For the most part, the movement in the novel as well as the film could be described as sequential—events and scenes are ordered in direct relation to each other. The exception, of course, would be a film like Alain Resnais' *Last Year at Marienbad* (1961), which deliberately eschews causality as well as psychological motivation. However, whether the order be A, B, C or C, B, A, the progression is usually straightforward. This tends to be true even if a film or novel opens with a conclusion (Orson Welles' *Citizen Kane* [1940] or Thornton Wilder's *Bridge of San Luis Rey* come to mind—both open with the protagonist's death); and even though the normal order has been reversed, the narrative will still tend to follow a relatively predictable, sequential path.

One of the exciting features of the film experience is its immediacy—the fact that the film is occurring *right now* before the audience's eyes. Although immediacy tends to promote greater involvement, it also creates certain problems for the film maker. Most of them center around considerations of time.

In order to describe a peculiar habit of one of his characters, a novelist might simply write: "Every day for six months at precisely eleven thirty-two, he would seat himself at a park bench on 27th Avenue and count the busses that passed." The reader unquestionably accepts the suggested duration of time; in other words, to the reader, it seems credible. For a film maker, this sentence would pose a problem. He would have to portray, visually and convincingly, the passage of six months in a relatively short segment of film. This would entail a number of shots of the man on the bench counting busses; it would also be necessary to indicate, within the shots, the passage of time. Typically, this would be accomplished by use of the background: trees blooming, leaves falling, then, finally, the stark, leafless, skeletal trees of winter. The changing attire of the man—short-sleeved shirt to jacket to overcoat—would also support this impression.

Conversely, a novelist might well devote an entire chapter to an event that actually took only seconds to transpire. A man nearly drowns. As he struggles to the surface and subsequently sinks again, the events of his life flit through his mind. Despite the fact that it might take an entire chapter to describe what thoughts race through his mind during this crisis, a reader would have no problem in accepting this chapter as credible. The film maker, however, cannot take advantage of this particular convention. If he moves the scene too rapidly, the viewer loses the density of the experience. If he takes too much time with the scene, its credibility is called into question. Robert Enrico, in his Cannes Film Festival Award-winning short film, *Occurrence at Owl Creek Bridge* (1961), does manage to successfully "stretch" the passage of a second or two into seventeen minutes. In order to do so, he has to introduce some ambiguities that make the viewer realize that time is being altered—but not why. The viewer believes that he is witnessing the miraculous escape of a man who was almost hanged, when in fact he is witnessing the internalized fantasy of a condemned man at the gallows.

It is a relatively easy task for the novelist to manipulate time. He can, for example, employ a narrator who tells a story from two vantage points simultaneously. The narrator can relate events that happened to him when he was seventeen as though he were again experiencing those same events in the present. The narrator, however, is now twenty-seven and the distance from the experience is ten years. Nevertheless, the writer can alternate between these two mentalities, the seventeen-year-old and the twenty-seven-year-old (as, for instance, John Updike does in his highly praised short story, *Flight*), with little difficulty. The film maker, however, will usually select one or the other (though not always, as in Ingmar Bergman's *Wild Strawberries* [1957]). Although it is possible to accompany the earlier scene with the voice of the older narrator, a strikingly different effect than the novelist's dual narrator is produced. The "voice over" (off-camera narration) tends to undermine the immediacy of the earlier scene.

There is, in addition, another curious feature that distinguishes time in a novel from time in a film: technically speaking, film time is always present tense. For example, open a conventional novel to a passage that deals with the past and the verbs alone will signal you that these events occurred some time ago. On the other hand, walk into a theater while a contemporary movie is in progress and try to determine whether you're watching past, present, future, or fantasy. Certainly, given enough time you would figure it out, but the point is that without the additional context, you'd have no way of knowing.

Not only is time employed differently in a film, but space is as well. In the novel, the reader brings his own experience to bear on the novelist's suggestions. If the novelist describes a building, the reader, having had the experience of visualizing a building, will tend to see a structure that conforms not only to the novelist's description but also to his own accumulated experience. Much of Wallace Stevens' poetry, for instance, is "about" or at least deals directly with this convention. In a film, however, the camera sees differently from the eye itself or the mind's eye, and the viewer tends to be more passive than the reader since the *conceptualization* of a scene is provided by the film.

This raises the entire question of conceptualization in the novel and the film. By its very nature, the film tends to be concrete and literal. The novel, on the other hand, is abstract and suggestive. The distinction is an important one, for it means that it is very difficult for the film to deal with abstractions. A brief example might serve to point up this distinction. In one of Macbeth's most famous speeches, he exclaims:

> Tomorrow and tomorrow and tomorrow
> Creeps in this petty pace from day to day,
> To the last syllable of recorded time;
> And all our yesterdays have lighted fools
> The way to dusty death. (Act V; sc. 5)

In the first two lines, Shakespeare has made use of personification; he describes an abstraction—tomorrow—as having the ability to creep, an activity that is usually limited to something animate. Similarly, in the following lines, he suggests that yesterdays (again, an abstraction) have "lighted fools the way to dusty death." The unusual juxtaposition of the abstract with the concrete produces a striking literary trope. A film maker obviously could have an actor deliver Macbeth's speech, but could not possibly film the kind of tropes that the speech includes. How, for example, could a film maker render the following in visual terms: a sea of troubles, a dusty nothing, liberty plucking authority by the nose, a dagger of the mind? The film, of course, through metaphors, similes, and symbols, does deal with abstractions, but it must necessarily render them in concrete images.

The literal-mindedness of the camera also produces other problems. Many writers (Nathaniel Hawthorne in *Young Goodman Brown*, Herman Melville in *Bartleby, the Scrivener*, and Franz Kafka in *The Trial*)[15] have successfully created characters who are representative figures of mankind. In each of these tales,

there is little physical description of the central character, with
the result that he becomes "universalized," an Everyman. The
camera, however, produces the opposite effect; it tends to wed
the character and the role forever. It is very difficult to imagine
La Strada (1954) without Giulietta Masina; *The Seventh Seal*
(1957) without Max Von Sydow; *The Graduate* (1968) without
Dustin Hoffman; and *Cries and Whispers* (1973) without Ingrid
Thulin, Harriet Andersson, Liv Ullman, and Kari Sylwan. Likewise, it is not enough for a character to experience a particular
scene as beautiful or threatening. In order to convince the
viewers, the scene must actually be filmed as beautiful or
threatening.

Finally, it should always be recognized that the film is a
multi-dimensional experience; it combines sight and sound with
movement. A film maker who is too "literary," who relies too
heavily on dialogue, will produce a film that is "talky." In fact,
at times there seems to be a basic conflict between literate or
complex language and visual imagery. In Anthony Harvey's *The
Lion in Winter* (1968), James Goldman's witty, literate screenplay provides the players with sparkling dialogue, yet the film
itself seems almost totally devoid of any memorable images.
Cartoonist Jules Feiffer, who wrote the screenplay for Mike
Nichols' *Carnal Knowledge* (1971), created a script that was
excessively talkative; in order to prevent the audience from being
distracted from the characters' speeches by competitive visuals,
Nichols was forced to constantly employ darkened and semi-
darkened lighting for the interior shots and extreme long shots
for the exteriors.

Likewise, a film maker who doesn't understand the languages
of vision and movement may end up producing a film that is
visually static. Some film makers attempt to avoid this by "opening up" the play with exterior shots and scenes that take place
away from the primary setting. Mike Nichols did this in *Who's
Afraid of Virginia Woolf?* (1966) with the opening shots of the
college campus and later, the roadhouse scene. William Freidkin's
Boys in the Band (1970), similarly, opened with a montage of
short scenes showing what the main characters were doing just
prior to their arrival at Michael's apartment.

The dramatist, of course, must confine his action to a relatively small area and restrict the movements of his characters

because of the spacial limitations of the stage. In a film, however, "all the world's a stage," and the film maker who ignores this creates a film that seems to the viewer to be unnecessarily restricted and confined.

REFERENCES

1. Joseph Roddy, "The Latest Model Mailer," *Look* (April 27, 1969), p. 25.
2. Erwin Panofsky, "Style and Medium in the Moving Pictures," *Film: An Anthology* (Berkeley: University of California, 1969), pp. 15–16.
3. Martin S. Day, *History of English Literature: 1660-1837* (Garden City, N.Y.: Doubleday, 1963), pp. 215–16.
4. Ian Watt, *The Rise of the Novel* (Berkeley: University of California Press, 1957), p. 48.
5. Ibid., p. 52.
6. Kenneth Macgowan, *Behind the Screen* (New York: Dell, 1965), p. 87.
7. Panofsky, p. 16.
8. Watt, p. 54.
9. A. R. Fulton, *Motion Pictures* (Norman, Okla.: University of Oklahoma Press, 1960), p. 79.
10. Susan Sontag, *Against Interpretation* (New York: Dell, 1966), p. 242.
11. Ezra Pound, *ABC of Reading* (New York: New Directions, 1960), p. 84.
12. Ibid., p. 21.
13. James Agee was one man who was at home both with the novel and the film. His *A Death in the Family* was posthumously awarded the Pulitzer Prize in 1957. He also found time to write five screenplays, the most famous of which was John Huston's *The African Queen* (1952). In addition, he was a film critic for *Time* and *The Nation,* and many people consider him one of the most perceptive critics who ever wrote.
14. Walter Ross, "Splicing Together Jean-Luc Godard," *Esquire* (July, 1969), p. 42.
15. Kafka's *The Trial* was brought to the screen in 1962; script and direction by Orson Welles.

Fig. II-A. Protagonist, Narrator, and Audience are all the same person.

Stream of Consciousness

FIRST PERSON

Fig. II-B. Protagonist and Narrator are the same person, but the audience is now someone external to the story.

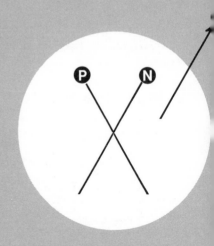

Narrator-Protagonist

FIRST PERSON

Fig. II-C. The Narrator is a person who witnessed the events of the story; the Protagonist is a second person; and the Audience again is outside the story.

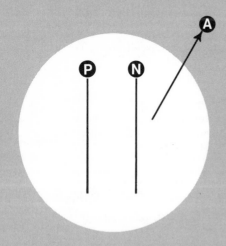

Observer, Witness,
Narrator-Participant

FIRST PERSON

Fig. II-D. The Narrator, now, is external to the events of the story; he has no personal stake in the outcome; his attitude toward the characters could be described as detached or indifferent. The Audience, like the Narrator, is external to the story.

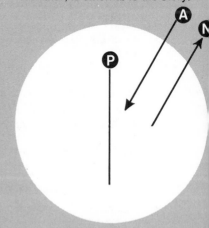

Detached Narrator

THIRD PERSON

2

POINT OF VIEW:

NARRATION AND CAMERA EYE

Fig. II-E
For a 16-mm camera, a
"normal" lens would
be 25 mm.

Fig. II-F
For a 16-mm camera, a
wide-angle lens would
be 12.5 mm.

Fig. II-G
For a 16-mm camera, a
telephoto lens would
be 150 mm.

Fig. II-H
An example of the extreme
wide-angle or "fish-eye"
lens filmed on a 16-mm
camera.

Fig. II-K
Frontlight.

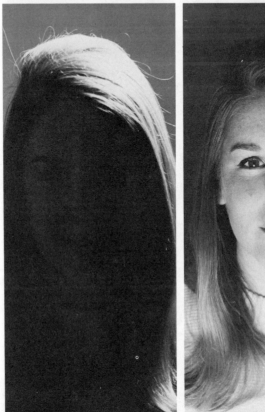

Fig. II-L
Backlight.

Fig. II-M
Sidelight.

Fig. II-N
Toplight.

Fig. II-O
Underlight.

Fig. II-P
Extreme Long Shot.

Fig. II-Q
Long Shot.

Fig. II-R
Medium Shot.

Fig. II-S
Close-up.

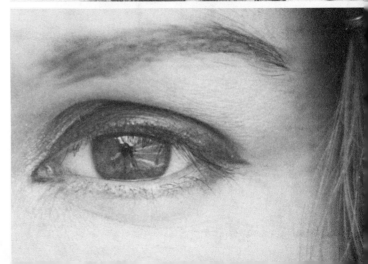

Fig. II-T
Extreme Close-up.

Fig. II-I
The telephoto lens, with its ability to compress space, is frequently used to dramatize the density of contemporary life.

American Stock Photos

Fig. II-J
Orson Welles' *Citizen Kane* (1941) makes extensive use of symbolism. Here, Kane's almost total estrangement from his second wife (played by Dorothy Comigore) is suggested by the physical distance that separates them and by the preponderance of "things" that have come between them. Gregg Toland, the Director of Photography, devised a lens system that could photograph, in sharp focus, anything from 18 inches away from the camera to infinity.

Courtesy of The Museum of Modern Art/Film Stills Archive

By restricting the point of view to only the pursued during the lengthy chase sequence in *Butch Cassidy and the Sundance Kid* (1969), director George Roy Hill forces the audience to identify with the protagonists.

Cecil B. De Mille made two versions of *The Ten Commandments:* the first appeared in 1923, and the second in 1956. Unquestionably, many people formed their conception of what the classical world looked like from De Mille's spectaculars.

THE TERM "point of view" refers to the perspective from which a particular story is told. Clearly, the choice of viewpoint is a significant decision for both novelist and film maker, since it determines *which* story is going to be told. A simple example may help to clarify how the narrator's viewpoint can affect a story.

A young girl meets her boyfriend at the house of a mutual friend, an older woman. At the meeting, the boy appears nervous. When questioned by the girl, he reveals his doubts about their relationship and suggests that they not see each other for a period of time. The girl, upset by his disclosure, begins to cry, but when he reaches out to comfort her, she jumps to her feet, rushes from the house and, in dashing across the street, is struck by an automobile. The boyfriend, the older woman, the driver of the car, ambulance attendants, a police officer, and a television reporter all hurry to the scene of the accident. The event—the girl being struck by the car—is an incontestable fact; the meaning and significance of what has happened are something else entirely. There are at least four different viewpoints concerning the impact of this event.

If the girl were to narrate the story, she would obviously describe the events as they appeared to her. She would express her joyful anticipation of the coming meeting, her disappointment when the boy began to express his feelings about the relationship, her grief as he suggested that they should not see each other, her shock as she fled the house, and, momentarily, her fear—before she was struck by the car. The story, perhaps, could be told as if it were a recording of her consciousness, as though every event were channeled through her mind: "His mouth is forming words that sound like 'separate for a while' and I begin to feel a numbness around my temples and forehead—my only thoughts are run! run!" Figure II-A (p. 22) illustrates this particular mode of narration. The circle here is intended to represent the "world" of the story. Notice that the protagonist (P), the narrator (N), and the audience (A) are all within this circle or world. But more importantly, notice that the P, N, and A overlap, indicating that the protagonist, narrator, and audience are all one and the same. In other words, the girl is the protagonist; she is narrating her own story; and she is apparently telling this story to herself.

Another obvious possibility is the boy. He might describe the same events to a friend on the day after the accident. He is now at a slight distance in time (one day) from what has happened, and his mental picture of the events is beginning to blur around the edges. Clearly, he is troubled by what has occurred as a result of his confession. Unlike the girl, however, who appeared to direct her remarks only to herself, the boy is speaking to a friend, whose presence influences both his choice of words and his manner of describing the event. His narrative is, in effect, a thinly disguised plea for forgiveness: "Of course, if I had thought for one minute that she would run out like that, I *never* would have told her."

The boy's point of view (see Figure II-B) is slightly but significantly different from the girl's. He has become our protagonist because he is at the center of the story now; we view and experience the events through his eyes. He is also the narrator, but the object of his narration—the friend—is placed outside the circle, as the friend had nothing to do with the events of the story. This same pattern occurs, of course, if the narrator is addressing a general, unspecified audience (as in a dramatic soliloquy, for example, or in a diary).

Another version of the story is that of the mutual friend. Although she is involved, she is further removed from the source of primary "truth" than the girl or boy, for she knows only what she has been able to directly observe and overhear. On the other hand, her view is more balanced than theirs; because she is well acquainted with both of the central figures, she can see both sides of the story. "I had known Karen from the time she was barely able to walk and Tom since he was five. . . ."

This friend (see Figure II-C) functions as a concerned but objective witness, thus enabling us to gain a better perspective on the central character or characters. And even though the speaker is still an "I," a personality who experiences and feels, it is clear that the central subject of the event and the narrator are not one and the same (note the separation of the P and the N). In the two previous examples, by contrast, the narrator and protagonist were identical. The story, as in example II-B, is being told to an audience who played no direct role in the events.

If a commentator for the local television news were to show his audience a film clip of the accident that night, another version of these same events would unfold. The audience would witness curious onlookers gathered around the periphery of the site where the girl was struck down; the camera would dutifully record the girl on a stretcher being lifted into the ambulance, the distressed driver of the automobile that struck her, and the unhappy boyfriend standing nearby. Accompanying the film, the audience would hear the voice of the news commentator saying something like: "Earlier this afternoon at the corner of Elm Street and 27th Avenue, a young girl identified as Miss Karen Turnbull of 242 West 8th Street was struck by a passing automobile." Now the voice—no longer an "I"—has become nearly colorless, depersonalized, recording only the relevant statistics: the who, what, when, where, and how of the accident. The significance of the event, for the television viewer, would center around the issue of who was at fault. The commentator, of course, draws no conclusion about this issue. The camera, like the voice, simply records what has happened.

With this particular point of view (see Figure II-D) the elements shift again. The girl remains the focus of attention, but the narrator was not on the scene, and—unlike the narrators in Figures A, B, and C—has no personal interest in the events he is describing. The audience's position remains the same as in Figures B and C, but in this case they are left to form their own opinions about what happened, since the narrator himself makes no judgment.

Unquestionably, there are other points of view from which this same story might be told. The driver of the car, who has been suddenly catapulted into the lives of the couple, is an obvious possibility. The story might have been told objectively (like the television-camera example) with the addition of the girl's thoughts, or the boy's, or both their thoughts, or even the thoughts of the mutual friend. The variations on this particular story are not infinite, but clearly there is a wide range of possibilities. The important thing to remember is that every time the point of view shifts, another, very different story is being told.

Novelists and film makers have long recognized that the meaning or truth of a story varies according to how it is being narrated. A case in point is Akira Kurosawa's *Rashomon* (1950); Kurosawa capitalizes on the subjectivity of the narrator by having the events of *Rashomon* related by four different people. Each time the story, which concerns a "rape" and violent death, is recounted, its meaning changes because each one of the narrators assumes responsibility for what has taken place. Kurosawa wisely never provides his audience with a "correct" interpretation. Rather, his film suggests that the "truth" or even the "reality" of an event is ultimately dependent upon who experiences it.

Although there are many notable exceptions, the short story and the novel usually adhere to a single point of view throughout, as a shift in point of view is apt to confuse or disorient the reader. The film maker, on the other hand, is likely to utilize several shifting points of view.

In the film, point of view must always be synonymous with camera eye, for the viewer has no choice except to witness what the camera perceives. Although point of view in film is considerably more limited than point of view in literature, film is capable of successfully depicting varying states of reality. Thus, some people in their twenties, and many in their thirties and forties, will always imagine the classical world like a Cecil B. De Mille spectacular, be it the Athens of Pericles or the Rome of Caligula.

At the turn of the century, movies were produced in much the same fashion as stage plays. The camera's position throughout the film was roughly the same as the fifth-row center of a theater audience, and the camera angle never varied from eye level. Actors and actresses made obvious entrances and exits from the movie set, the action was blocked out in advance as in a stage production, and the camera ran without interruption until a scene had concluded.

Then, during the 1920s, a number of film makers (notably F. W. Murnau, E. A. Dupont, and G. W. Pabst) began to extend the vocabulary and techniques of the narrative film. The discovery that the camera can move—right and left (a pan); up and down (a tilt); inward (a close-up); away (a long shot)—initiated an artistic revolution in film making. Before the liberation of the camera, everything that was filmed corresponded roughly to the objective, detached narrator of Figure II-D. Freeing the camera caused the frame (perimeter of the screen) to begin expanding and contracting as the camera moved closer to or further away from the subject. The camera could now begin to exert the kind of artistic control over its material and the spectators' emotions that had usually been associated only with the novelist and the short-story writer.

There is a scene in D. W. Griffith's *Intolerance* (1916) that illustrates how the moving camera can control a viewer's emotional response. Mae Marsh is in the courtroom watching her husband being tried for murder. She attempts to bolster his spirits by smiling reassuringly during the proceedings. However, in one brief close-up, Griffith cuts to her hands; they are not visible to her husband, and she twists them nervously. Instantly, the viewer knows that she is tense, and frightened for her husband. A playwright, it should be noted, would have no equivalent for such a technique.

Similarly, in David Lean's *Lawrence of Arabia* (1962), there is a scene in which Lawrence, against the advice and warnings of men who know the dangers of the desert much better than he does, elects to return to a particularly desolate area in order to rescue a comrade who had fallen from his mount the night before. Though the audience can certainly appreciate the risk Lawrence is running, the real impact is not fully experienced until the camera pulls steadily back from the scene in an extreme long shot, revealing the frail, solitary figure of Lawrence pitted against the enormous barrenness of the desert.

Not long after the discovery of camera movement, film makers began to discover that the camera does not have to be a passive witness to the world, but can assume an active role in the depiction of reality. The camera began adopting vantage points that literally corresponded with the narrator's point of view. Film makers found, for example, that they were able to simulate a child's view of the world simply by altering the height of the camera—if it were lowered and angled upward, adults and objects could be made to appear enormous.

Although the placing of the camera can powerfully suggest, as well as comment upon, a character or scene, it still restricts the camera to observable reality. Another significant breakthrough in the film experience occurred when film makers began to examine subjective states of reality—dreams, memories, fantasies, and altered states of consciousness. As they began to investigate and explore various levels of subjective reality, they learned to reflect the mind's alternation between fantasy and reality. Many of these early attempts to convey subjective states of mind, however, were blatantly staged. A character might stand meditatively before the camera; the audience would see his image beginning to ripple, and then observe the same character, now much younger, at some point in his past. This technique is, of course, the flashback—an attempt to indicate the effect of the past on the present. Contemporary film makers no longer feel the necessity to "introduce" flashbacks, memories, and fantasies; they simply let them occur.

At the start of Sidney Lumet's *The Pawnbroker* (1965), for example, there are many extremely rapid cuts that reveal the agonized recollections of an elderly Jew who had spent a period of time in a concentration camp. Initially, the viewer is totally unprepared for these memories. The pawnbroker (played by Rod Steiger) is sitting comfortably in a lawn chair in the backyard of a suburban home, and suddenly memories of the concentration-camp experience flit through his mind. The cuts are so quick (probably as short as five or six frames) that the viewer is not even quite sure of what he has seen. It is only through an accumulation of these shots that the viewer begins to piece together the gruesome reality of the pawnbroker's past.

Robert Enrico, director of *An Occurrence at Owl Creek Bridge,* devotes the greater proportion of the film to a fantasized escape by the protagonist. Unlike Lumet, Enrico does indicate to the audience that a distortion of reality is being introduced. The sound track is slowed down, the Union soldiers on the bridge move in slow motion. But only at the conclusion of the film, when the viewer finally realizes that what he has seen are escape fantasies experienced by a man a few seconds before his death, does he grasp the significance of the distortions that have been introduced.

An English film, John Schlesinger's *Billy Liar* (1963), alternates between the fantasies and the reality of the life of a young clerk in the undertaker's business. At one particularly frustrating point in the film, Billy imagines himself dressed in a trooper's uniform, machine-gunning his tormentors. More recently, Roger Corman's *The Trip* (1967) and Dennis Hopper's *Easy Rider* (1969) have attempted to portray the altered mental states produced by mind-expanding drugs. Numerous psychedelic effects are introduced by means of rapid cutting, distortional lenses, and the use of various kinds of film stocks.

Each of the techniques described above—the memory, the dream, the fantasy, and the drug experience—are the film's equivalent for the stream-of-consciousness technique described in

Figure II-A. Each is an attempt to reveal the inner workings of an individual's mind, and each suggests the complex interplay between illusion and reality.

The camera as narrator-protagonist (Figure II-B) is an unusual technique, but it has been used, most notably in Robert Montgomery's 1946 adaptation of Raymond Chandler's *Lady in the Lake*. In this instance, the viewer "becomes" the protagonist; what the camera is "seeing" the protagonist is seeing, and since the viewer is seeing through the "eyes" of the protagonist, he, in a sense, becomes the protagonist. Arthur Knight, in *The Liveliest Art*, discusses an early application of the first-person technique in Reuben Mamoulian's *Dr. Jekyll and Mr. Hyde* (1932):

> . . . the entire first reel was shot in the first-person technique, the camera assuming the identity of Dr. Jekyll. From that position we see his hands as he plays the organ, the shadow of his head upon the music rack. When Jekyll is ready to go out, the butler hands hat, cloak and cane directly to the camera.[2]

This technique seems to be most effective when it is used sparingly. Unlike the short story and novel, the film must, in a sense, efface the narrator as both reflecting personality and, to a large extent, participant in the action (as in the *Dr. Jekyll and Mr. Hyde* example), in order to use the point of view shown in Figure II-B.

Although film can employ the "interested observer" technique (Figure II-C), many of the same problems that plague the first-person narrator hamper the narrator-participant. It would be easy enough to imagine a group of men gathered about a table in a tavern listening to the narrator. Again, the camera could be placed in such a manner to convey the impression that it is the narrator. The men at the table look attentively at the camera; occasionally clouds of smoke obscure the camera as the narrator lights his pipe. The audience hears the voice of the narrator: "I want to tell you about a remarkable young man that I met in South Africa last year." At this point the narrator-participant is fulfilling the same function as his fictional equivalent: he is a personality, shaping the responses of the listener ("a remarkable young man"), indicating to his audience that the story is the young man's and not his own ("I want to tell you about . . ."), and it is clear that he is telling the story. However, when the story shifts to the past, as it must, the narrator-participant will either be in or out of the story. If he is in, then the audience loses the editorializing of the narrator: "I thought it was strange when he told me that he would be leaving for Zanzibar the following Thursday, but only much later would I discover the real significance of his sudden departure." Here, it is apparent that there are two mentalities operating within the same narrator: (1) what the narrator-as-fallible-human thought at the time the event occurred, and (2) what he now knows as a result of further experience or information. The film maker can, of course, return the audience to the table in the tavern, but obviously he must interrupt the action to do so. If the narrator-participant is out of the action, then the same limitations that restricted the first-person narrator mentioned above will apply.

An objective or detached narrator (Figure II-D) is most frequently used by the film maker, for several reasons. First, this technique maximizes the camera's narrative potential while minimizing its limitations. The camera can view things microscopically, as in the case of an extreme close-up, or it can shift to a vast overview of its subject with a panoramic shot or even an aerial view. Thus, it is able to achieve a kind of omniscience that is frequently associated with the objective or detached narrator in fiction. There is usually no editorializing, except for selectivity, and the audience is simply shown the events of the story. Utilizing this point of view allows the camera far more latitude than the exclusive use of any one point of view. For example, if the camera is being used to record the protagonist's point of view, then it is obviously restricted to what that individual would be capable of perceiving. To use an aerial shot, the director would have to put the protagonist in an airplane; to have the protagonist see himself, the director would have to use a mirror, a picture of the protagonist, or a dream or flashback sequence. With the detached or objective narrator (a technique that is sometimes called the "camera eye"), the camera can conceivably adopt any point of view—take on the powers of a god-like narrator, become capable of viewing the action regardless of time or geographical limitations. It can, for example, show a character in the living room of his home and suddenly shift to an aerial shot of the community in which the character lives. Likewise, if the character is thinking about his brother who is traveling through Europe, the camera can show the audience the brother riding on a train through southern France.

Most of the films that an audience views today combine a variety of points of view, but the basis of the narrational technique is usually the detached, objective narrator. However, a film that employs *only* this technique lacks intimacy; working at a distance, it curtails the viewer's involvement. Conversely, a film that restricts itself to a first-person subjective narration imposes unnecessary limitations on the story—the experience is much like trying to view the world through the eyepiece of a telescope: undoubtedly interesting, but constricting.

It cannot be emphasized too strongly that point of view is of critical importance to the artist, because it determines not only which story is to be told but, to a great extent, how it will be told. Point of view calls to mind the parable of the six blind men who attempt to describe the elephant: the man who seizes upon the trunk remarks that the elephant is very much like a snake; the man who feels the elephant's side disagrees because, to him, the elephant is more like a wall; and another, who is touching the elephant's leg, argues that both of his companions are in error for the elephant is most assuredly like a tree trunk. Clearly, where each of the men is positioned in relation to the elephant determines the "story" he will narrate.

Once the film maker has determined which story he wishes to tell, he must then consider how that story must be told. Since his story is to be related in a visual language, he must consider what images will best convey it.[3] Manipulation of visual images involves six factors: (1) the choice of camera lens; (2) the kind, intensity, and direction of light selected; (3) the type of film stock to be employed; (4) the angle of the camera in relation to the subject; (5) the distance of the subject from the camera; and (6) the speed at which the camera is being run when the subject is filmed.

The "heart" of any camera is its lens, for it is the lens which determines the kind of image that will be transferred from the outside world onto the film. The lens is frequently referred to as the "eye" of the camera. This can be a useful analogy, for the lens in many ways does emulate the functions of the human eye. On the other hand, the analogy is somewhat misleading because the camera lens records the world in a slightly different fashion than the eye. The human eye is a much more versatile lens than the lens of the camera; it permits a person to change his focus almost instantly from an object only a few inches away to another object as far away as the horizon. Also, the eye takes in a larger area of information than most camera lenses because an individual's field of vision is always roughly 180 degrees, even though a large percentage of the scene is typically composed of two dimly perceived peripheries, with most attention centered on a relatively small area. For example, if an individual is scanning a crowd for a friend, he is only faintly aware of the vast panorama of people, because his area of concentration is limited to five or six at a time; if he simply took stock of the crowd as a whole, he would be seeing very differently.

A film maker has at his disposal many different kinds of lenses, each of which will significantly alter the way in which a given shot will be perceived. The choice of lens is usually determined by two basic considerations: (1) the magnitude (size) of the image desired, and (2) the effect of the lens on "normal" perspective.

Consider the changes that take place when different lenses are placed on a 16-millimeter camera (like most classroom projectors). For a 16-mm camera, a "normal" lens would be a 25-mm. *Normal*, as indicated by the quotation marks, is a relative term. A 16-mm camera equipped with a normal lens will record objects pretty much as the viewer would ordinarily perceive them, if he did not attempt to narrow or enlarge the field of vision. In any given shot, the sizes of the objects will appear in ordinary perspective; objects close to the camera will appear larger than objects farther away.

Imagine a 16-mm camera set up on a lawn. About fifty feet in front of the camera, there is a girl sitting; behind and to the right of the girl is a building (see Figure II-E, p. 58). Shooting this scene with the 25-mm lens would reveal all of the girl in the center of the frame; behind the girl and to her right, the viewer would see, in normal perspective, the building; the grassy area in front of and behind the girl would also appear in a normal perspective. Everything in the scene would be in relatively sharp focus (i.e., there would be little fuzziness or blurring, except in those areas near the horizon).

Now, without moving the camera from its position, the film maker replaces the "normal" lens with a 12.5-mm lens—a "wide angle" (Figure II-F). Even though nothing but the lens has been altered, the change in the recorded image is rather striking. The distance from the foreground to the background appears to have been elongated; the grassy area in front of the girl seems wider, the building behind her seems further away, and the images in general seem smaller. Once again, all of the images seem to be in sharp focus.

If the film maker again changes the lens, replacing the wide angle with a 150-mm long lens—the "telephoto"—the picture is significantly altered. The telephoto lens (Figure II-G) functions much as a telescope does—it magnifies the image. The viewer now sees only the girl, who appears so close that he could reach out and touch her. Besides the magnification of the image, the viewer notices that some other changes have taken place. The building behind the girl is not only blurry, but appears to have moved closer to her. The grassy area between them doesn't seem to be as wide as it was before; the grass also looks as though it were a hazy carpet of green. To the viewer, the girl is easily the most dominant focal point in this shot—the grass and building seem very subdued in comparison.

If the film maker were interested in producing an exaggerated distortional effect in this scene, he might use still another lens—the extreme wide-angle lens, or, as it is sometimes called, the "fish-eye." Using this lens (Figure II-H), the scene, to the viewer, would appear to resemble a globe; the corners of the frame would be rounded and the area of information (what the viewer sees in the frame) would be increased. The shot would reveal all of the girl and the building behind her, including part of the sky. The picture itself, however, would look distorted; the images in the center of the frame would seem to curve backward at the edges and bulge inward at the center.

Each time the lens is changed, the viewer is forced to view the scene differently. His response to the image is obviously shaped according to the way in which it has been presented to him. Which lens the film maker will select is predetermined by what he wants to do with the scene.

If the scene is a dream or a fantasy, the film maker might choose to shoot it with the fish-eye or the telephoto lens. Either lens would impart an air of unreality to the scene that would be appropriate to this subject matter. But the extreme distortion of the fish-eye lens would also introduce a visual grotesqueness. If the lawn were the site of a traumatic incident, this grotesqueness might well be appropriate. On the other hand, if the lawn represents a pleasant memory, the film maker would probably want to avoid this effect. The telephoto lens with its critical depth of field would select the area of focus, while lending a somewhat romantic atmosphere to the scene. The less dominant aspects of the scene would blend into an impressionistic blur, while the girl would stand out in sharp relief. In other words, the eye of the viewer would immediately gravitate to the girl.

With the telephoto lens, the girl is selected from the overall context of the scene. This might easily be an appropriate shot if the girl has a definite relationship to the protagonist. But if the film maker wishes the girl to be only a part of the total context—the scene as a whole—he might decide to employ the wide-angle lens. The wider lens would render a stronger feeling of place because it would take in a broader area.

Lens selection can also be used to impart additional meaning to a given shot. The telephoto lens, with its ability to compress space, has frequently been used with great success to indicate the density of contemporary life. Shooting a crowded sidewalk or street with this lens produces a dramatic effect—the people or the automobiles appear to be virtually on top of each other (see Figure II-I). As might be expected, this lens will also affect movement.

The camera equipped with a telephoto lens will also visually affect movement. Because of its ability to compress space, the lens makes it seem that there is less movement taking place than there actually is. This, of course, can be a particularly appropriate dramatic effect on certain occasions. For example, in Mike Nichols' *The Graduate,* one scene shows Benjamin running to catch up with Elaine; though he's running extremely hard, the telephoto lens makes it appear that he's really getting nowhere. In a similar fashion, this lens also has the effect of "flattening out" an image and making real spatial differences appear uniform. In George Roy Hill's *Butch Cassidy and the Sundance Kid* (1969), the protagonists do everything they can to elude the specially formed posse; no matter what tricks they execute, however, the posse appears to be exactly the same distance away whenever they look back. Their sense of frustration, then, as well as the posse's dogged pursuit, is visually conveyed by the telephoto lens.

The telephoto lens has also been used to rivet the audience's attention on a certain aspect of a shot. Imagine a camera set up in the living room of an apartment, slightly behind and above a couch. The foreground—the area where the couch is located—is not in focus, hence blurred. In the background, in sharp focus, the audience views the wall of the apartment that faces the hall-way. After a while, the audience hears a key turning in the lock, then watches the door open into the apartment. A woman enters. At this moment, the entire scene comes into sharp focus, revealing a man hidden behind the couch. A scene that had previously seemed quite mundane now takes on an aura of tension and expectation. In this example, the foreground was used to comment on the background.

A film maker can easily reverse this technique and use the background to comment on the foreground. A married woman is clandestinely meeting her lover in a small café. The critical focus of the camera is on the couple, who are earnestly engaged in conversation at their table. The background—the rest of the café—is out of focus. The audience watches the couple for a minute, then the camera changes focus, the foreground becomes blurred, and the background comes into focus, revealing the husband of the woman seated at a table in the rear of the restaurant. The relaxed atmosphere of the café, for the audience, suddenly becomes charged.

As might be expected, the wide-angle lens would tend to reverse the visual effects of the telephoto or long lens. The most frequent use of the wide-angle involves outdoor shots, for the lens is capable of taking in wider areas of information—it is clearly better suited for sweeping panoramic scenes. But, like the tele-photo lens, it can also be employed to convey additional information to an interior shot.

In regard to movement, a wide-angle lens will create the illusion that more of it is occurring than is actually the case. This effect could be very useful in certain instances. In the previously mentioned example of the runner and the pursuer, the film maker might wish to emphasize the rapid, relentless pace of the man who is chasing the runner. By filming the pursuer with the wide-angle lens, he could make it appear that the pursuer was moving at a tremendous rate of speed; this, of course, would also have the effect of emphasizing the plight of the runner.

Whereas the telephoto lens will make things appear to be closer together than they actually are, the wide-angle lens will make them seem farther apart. This lens has the effect of "stretching out" an image. Again, it can influence the way in which a viewer will perceive a shot. If this lens is used in a large room occupied by only a few people, it would make the people appear farther apart from each other than they actually are. Were the film maker attempting to indicate the isolation and loneliness of these people, judicious use of the wide-angle lens would definitely lend visual support to this idea (see Figure II-J).

By now it should be clear that the way in which a visual image is recorded has a great deal to do with meaning in a film. The visual effect that a particular lens produces in an image can easily be as important as what occurs or what is said in a given scene. In some instances, what the camera reveals to the audience might even be more important than what the characters are saying to each other. For example, were the film maker to use the wide-angle lens in a large drawing room with only two people present, a husband and his wife, the audience would see the couple as being far apart physically. If the husband tells the wife, "I feel close to you," the audience would tend not to believe his words, for there is clearly a discrepancy between what he is saying and what the audience is witnessing. The choice of lenses in a given shot can nearly always be related to meaning.

The manner in which a shot is lighted is also related to meaning. From time immemorial, people have been influenced by the presence or absence of light. A dark, gloomy day is frequently felt as "depressing," whereas a bright, sunny day is experienced as "uplifting." And poets have always made use of light to render a mood or an atmosphere that is appropriate to their subjects. Daybreak is frequently related to new life; late afternoon to the waning years; night to death. Dylan Thomas' great tribute to his dying father, *Do No Go Gentle into that Good Night,* presents a striking poetic example of the metaphorical use of night-as-death.

The film maker tends to use light in much the same way as the poet. For instance, the final scene of Gilbert Cates' *I Never Sang for My Father* (1970) deals with a son's attempt to convince his widowed eighty-year-old father that he should leave his two-generation home in White Plains, New York, and join the son and his wife in California. The father refuses and is indignant that the son will not remain on the East Coast. The son realizes that nothing more can be done, and drives away from the house. The camera, however, remains stubbornly fixed on the darkened house with the solitary light in the upstairs window. The image becomes a freeze frame, but so subtly that the change is almost undetectable. Then the light winks off. Clearly, the combination of the freeze frame and the extinguished light are meant to suggest the figurative death of the father.

Basically, there are two different types of lighting—natural and artificial. Natural lighting, of course, is provided by the sun, artificial lighting by electricity. Each may be used by itself or in combination. Again, the choice of lighting is determined by the way the film maker wishes the scene to be perceived. Natural lighting, for example, is not a static quantity; it is constantly changing. At sunrise and at sunset, there is usually a predominance of red tones, thus imparting a feeling of warmth to the image. At noon, on the other hand, the light tends to become flat and colorless, creating a quite different kind of visual effect.

Not only the color, but also the intensity of the light, changes during the day—a late-afternoon sun will cast long shadows and darken certain areas of the image. Thus, by controlling the degree of light intensity in a given scene the film maker can create a certain mood or atmosphere. Light comedies are usually photographed in what is known as "high key" lighting, that is, lighting that is bright and unshadowed. The bright lighting is appropriate in broadly satirical films such as Peter Bogdanovich's *What's Up, Doc?* (1972) or musical comedies such as William Wyler's *Funny Girl* (1968). On the other hand, most horror movies employ "low key" lighting in order to create dark, heavily shadowed visuals and a feeling of mystery and foreboding. Indeed, shadows are often used as the symbolic embodiment of villainy. Tod Browning's *Dracula* (1931) and Jacques Tourneur's *Cat People* (1942) —where the cat people are shown only as shadows, leaving the rest to the viewer's imagination—are especially effective in this regard.

Obviously, the use of high- and low-key lighting is not restricted to comedies and horror films. The melancholy films of Ingmar Bergman, predictably, make extensive use of low-key lighting; for instance, *The Seventh Seal* (1957) and *The Magician* (1959). However, both Federico Fellini (*La Dolce Vita* [1959]) and Alain Resnais (*Last Year at Marienbad* [1961]) have successfully employed high-key lighting in films that are serious and somber.

As might be expected, white light is not a homogeneous substance, but rather a mixture of seven colors: red, orange, yellow, green, blue, indigo, and violet. The reds are the strongest rays in the spectrum, whereas the violets are the weakest. By using a filter, a film maker can, to a great extent, control and alter the visual impact of a given shot (this holds true for black-and-white films as well as color). A filter, typically a piece of dyed glass that is placed in front of the camera's lens, performs a negative function, that is, it removes certain rays in the color spectrum. Effective employment of a filter can make a significant contribution to a visual composition.

For example, if a film maker were to use a red filter in an outdoor shot, the filter would considerably darken the sky, producing an ominous and threatening effect. On the other hand, a green filter would have a tendency to increase color contrast and yet soften the light contrasts. Richard Lester, a British film maker, made suggestive use of a filter in *Petulia* (1967). One scene shows a couple shopping in an all-night grocery store in San Francisco. The store is one of those emporiums that are crammed with a plethora of canned goods, instant foods, and cellophaned vegetables. Its interior is dominated by whites; walls and ceiling, display cases, uniforms, goods, and check-out stands all suggest an otherwordly atmosphere. Lester employs a filter that causes the shot to be dominated by blue tones. The result is eerie: a relatively ordinary grocery store suddenly becomes an alien, cold, almost frighteningly dehumanized landscape—an exact counterpart, in fact, of the spiritual wastelands Petulia, her husband, and her lover inhabit. Thus, the use of filters as a means of controlling light values can influence the viewer's understanding of a shot.

Light, of course, always emanates from a source, be it the sun or a floodlight. Again, how that light strikes a subject is critically important; for, like the lenses and the filters, it will determine how a viewer will perceive any given image.

Basically, there are five directions from which a subject can be illuminated: frontlight, backlight, toplight, sidelight, and underlight. In each case, the source of light is at a different angle to the subject. An easy and instructive experiment would be to make your own study of the effect of lighting on a subject. In a semi-darkened room (a bathroom would serve nicely), stand before a mirror with a desk lamp or flashlight. Hold the light directly in front of your face (frontlight—see Figure II-K) and study the effects of the light on your face. Notice that your face appears to be normally lighted, that the image in the mirror is, in the main, unshadowed and complimentary. Any shadows cast by the light fall behind your face and are, for the most part, unnoticed.

Now move the light directly in back of your head (backlight —Figure II-L). You will notice that there is a rim of light around your hair and the sides of your face—visually the effect is much like a halo. But notice also that your face is now evenly shadowed, as the light source is coming from behind. If the light source is then moved to the side (sidelight—Figure II-M), another different effect is created. Your face is now evenly split into half light and half dark.

Moving the illumination directly over your head (toplight— Figure II-N) again alters the image in the mirror. This time all of the hair is brightly illuminated, but only a portion of the face. The prominent features—the bridge of the nose, perhaps the cheekbones as well—receive a fraction of the spillover light, but the remainder of the face is deeply shadowed.

Finally, move the light beneath your chin and angle it upward (underlight—Figure II-O). You will recognize this style of lighting almost immediately. The shadows are cast unnaturally upward, making the face appear unnatural; the upper part of the nose is deeply shadowed, as are the eye sockets, and the top of the head is very dark. This kind of lighting is most frequently seen in horror movies.

Varying the light in this manner not only significantly alters the visual impact of a shot, but also helps to reveal character. Ralph Stephenson and J. R. Debrix, in *The Cinema As Art*, comment upon the effect of light on the human face:

> Lighting from above spiritualizes a subject and gives it a solemn or angelic look . . . or an air of youth and freshness. Lighting from below imparts a feeling of unease and gives a wicked or unearthly appearance. Lighting from the side gives relief and solidity to a face, but may make it ugly and show the lines. It may indicate an ambiguous personality, half good, half bad, symbolically half

light, half shade. Lighting from in front blurs any faults, flattens
relief, softens modelling, makes the face more beautiful, but takes
away its character. Coming from behind, lighting idealizes a
subject, giving it an ethereal quality. This sort of lighting is a
modern version of the halo of the saints or the aura of a medium.[4]

It is evident that the way in which a subject is lighted is
bound to affect a viewer's response. It is less apparent, however,
that the very type of film selected will also influence the viewer's
perception. The images are recorded on film stock, which is
essentially composed of long strips of a plastic-like base material
called celluloid or cellulose acetate; on top of this base material
is a coating, an emulsion that contains particles which actually
record the image. There are several different widths of film stock:
8 mm, 16 mm, 35 mm, 70 mm and larger. Most home movies are
shot on 8-mm or super-8 film stock; classroom projectors typically
use 16-mm film; the larger sizes are usually restricted to commercial productions. In general, the larger the film width, the
better quality the projected image.

In addition to size, the film maker must also consider the
film's sensitivity to light, for this will usually determine the visual
texture of his image. A so-called "fast" film requires less light to
record an image, whereas a "slow" film requires more. However,
when a "fast" film is used, it typically reveals a certain amount of
graininess in the projected image. A newspaper photograph is
usually grainy—the image appears "rough" and lacks subtle color
differentiation. "Slow" film, on the other hand, produces a much
more even, polished image.

Choice of film stock is intimately related to the intentions of
the film maker. If he were attempting to film a remake of Norman
McLeod's 1947 *Secret Life of Walter Mitty* (based on the James
Thurber story), he would certainly be faced with the problem
of visually indicating Mitty's sudden leaps from reality to fantasy.
In Thurber's story, almost any kind of sensory suggestion—the
monotonous movement of the windshield wipers, a car backfiring
—is enough to trigger one of Mitty's fantasies. One method of
resolving this problem might be to use two different kinds of film
—"slow" as well as "fast" film stock. The slower stock would
record reality more "naturally"—the range from black to white
would be filled with all the subtle intermediate shades of gray.
The faster film, on the other hand, would point up the unreality

of Mitty's fantasies because many of the in-between gray tones would be lost.

Because a faster film requires less light, it is frequently selected by documentarists and television cameramen (a large percentage of the six o'clock news is filmed material). Both the newsmen and the documentarists must rely heavily on natural available light so they can move with the action, unencumbered by bulky lighting equipment. Audiences have grown so used to witnessing documentaries and news stories on high-contrast, grainy footage that they associate this kind of film stock with "realistic" photography. Obviously, a film maker who is dealing "realistically" with a subject will keep this association in mind. John Cassavetes' *Faces* (1968), which brutally depicts the frustration and despair of a middle-class couple, makes extensive use of "fast" film stock. The result is a film that seems spontaneous and unrehearsed.

Prior to the 1960s, color stock was restricted, for the most part, to certain kinds of productions: typically musicals, sweeping historical pageants, and slick comedies. More serious films were, almost without exception, photographed in black and white. There were several reasons for this: first, color stock was more expensive, and producers displayed a marked reluctance to invest additional money in color without being relatively sure that the production was going to be a popular (i.e., financial) success. Many of the productions of the serious film makers were not only frankly experimental in nature, but were also apt to deal with subjects that a general audience would find "uninteresting" or even "distasteful." As a result, many of the early films of today's great film makers, when first shown, were viewed by relatively small audiences.

But money was not the only reason that film makers avoided color. Color stock was much more difficult to control than black and white. Use of color not only required high-intensity lighting, but also precluded subtle gradations of tone. Hence, artistic control over visuals was radically diminished. There was also an unspoken law among film makers that black and white was a more appropriate vehicle for the "serious" film. Color, on the other hand, was deemed flashy and garish.

Today, most of this has changed. The cost differential between black and white and color is not as great as it was before. Technical advances have made color much more susceptible to artistic control. And finally, an ever-increasing number of film makers such as Bergman (*Cries and Whispers* [1973]); Fellini (*Juliet of the Spirits* [1964] and *Fellini Roma* [1972]); Antonioni (*Red Desert* [1964], *Blow-Up* [1967] and *Zabriskie Point* [1970]); Kubrick (*Clockwork Orange* [1972]); Widerberg (*Elvira Madigan* [1967]); and Pasolini (*Teorema* [1968]) have produced "serious" films in color.

In recent years, a virtual revolution has been taking place in the film industry with regard to the use of color. It is not uncommon to see black and white used in a film that is predominantly in color. Frequently, black and white stock will be printed on color stock, creating unusual tones and textures. Experimentalists, such as Stan VanDerBeek, have discovered that video tape can be subjected to a series of color wash processes and then transferred to film—and the result is an entire new range of color combinations and image qualities. Still, creative use of color in film is a relatively unexplored area.

Earlier in this chapter, it was suggested that the angle at which a camera is placed will significantly influence an audience's perception of an image. Basically, camera angle refers to the relationship between the subject and the camera. Most camera angles start from a norm of an eye-level view. That is to say, if the camera is placed below eye level and angled upward, this would be designated as a *low angle*, whereas anything above eye level, angled downward, would be described as a *high angle*. There are, of course, gradations: a camera placed on the ground and angled upward would represent an *extreme low angle;* a shot from a high rooftop of the street would be considered an *extreme high angle*.

Consider, for instance, the opening shot of Frank Schaffner's *Patton* (1970). The background is totally dominated by an enormous American flag, and when George C. Scott, who plays Patton, moves into the foreground he lookes like a carving from Mount Rushmore that has suddenly come to life. This effect—which immediately makes the audience see Patton as the stuff legends are made of—is almost exclusively the result of camera angle. Reversal of camera angle would, predictably, produce the opposite effect. A character who is repeatedly photographed from above appears weak and inconsequential.

Camera angle has also been used to emphasize an effect or a condition. The struggle of a wounded man crawling up a hill is dramatic in itself, but angling the camera so as to accentuate the steepness of the hill makes his task seem even more arduous. Similarly, if a runaway wagon containing a helpless child is plunging down a hillside, exaggeration of camera angle can contribute to the tension.

Another important factor to consider is how the film maker delineates space in his films. In D. W. Griffith's *Intolerance*, for instance, a wealthy industrialist decides to reduce the wages of his workers because he believes they spend money on unnecessary frivolities such as dancing. He plans to contribute the amount of money by which he is reducing their wages to his s] inster sister's "Do Good" fund in order that the money be put to "better uses." Because a wide social gulf divides his life from that of his workers, the owner can neither understand nor sympathize with their needs. Thus, Griffith often shows the industrialist seated behind a massive and imposing desk in the center of an otherwise empty office. Visually, the effect is that of an island in the midst of an ocean; Griffith is graphically portraying the industrialist as a man apart, aloof and alone. By contrast, Griffith visually depicts the workers in a group, both at work and at play. Thus, simple spatial relationships can be utilized to comment upon or underwrite thematic issues.

Distance from camera to subject also influences the way an audience will experience an image. Fundamentally, these distances are divided into three broad areas: the close-up, the medium shot, and the long shot (see Figures II-P through II-T). The *long shot*, for example, might show a girl, full length, by a building. A *medium shot* would show the girl from approximately the waist up—this shot, of course, would bring the viewer much closer to the subject. A *close-up*, more intimate yet, might show only the girl's face. As with camera angles, there are gradations that exist within these broad areas. An *extreme long shot* might take in much more of the area surrounding the girl; it could, for example, indicate that the girl is in front of an office. The extreme long shot contributes a stronger sense of place. Finally, in an *extreme close-up*, the entire screen would be filled with the eye of the girl.

Whether a given shot is considered a long shot or a close-up is a relative matter. If the subject is the Empire State Building, then a long shot might take in the entire building, whereas an extreme close-up could be an item as large as a single window.

The selection of any one shot usually touches upon the meaning of a film. In some instances, the film maker has little choice in shot selection, for the shot may be dictated by the action of a scene. If he wishes to show a popular insurrection, he must necessarily film long wide-angle shots of the crowd, or the impact of the number of people participating is lost. Likewise, if a character, in a moment of excitement, reveals some startling information about himself to another character, the audience naturally wants to observe the other character's response to this revelation, and the film maker would almost have to show a close-up of his face.

Otherwise, shot selection in a film is usually determined by the kind of story that is being told. A love story or a psychological study of a character, for example, would be characterized by extensive use of intimate photography (i.e., extreme close-ups and close-ups); the long shot or even the medium shot, in this kind of narrative, would tend to erode the feeling of intimacy.

Ingmar Bergman's films, for instance, utilize a great many close-ups and medium-close shots. Bergman's concern, typically, is with one individual or a couple of individuals; an "intimate" camera is appropriate to his complex, subjective, psychological approach. On the other hand, films that are essentially satirical portraits of society, such as Stanley Kubrick's *Dr. Strangelove* (1964), or Richard Attenborough's *Oh! What a Lovely War* (1969), work at a considerable distance from their characters because Kubrick and Attenborough are depicting types.

An audience's response to an image will certainly be affected by the speed at which the subject has been photographed. By showing a man running down the street in "fast motion," a film maker can cause the runner to appear ludicrous; but the same man running the same way, photographed in "slow motion," could be made to appear graceful, almost "poetic" in his movements.

Fast motion, which is produced by reducing the speed at which motion is usually photographed and projecting it at normal speed, exaggerates the jerkiness and clumsiness of any movement. As a technique, it was a comic staple of the early silent films and it enabled film makers to stage narrow escapes and near-accidents without actually endangering anyone's life. Although fast motion is not used as extensively today as it once was, it is still occasionally employed to augment the comedy of a scene as in Tony Richardson's *Tom Jones* (1963), Richard Lester's *The Knack* (1965), and Sam Peckinpah's *The Ballad of Cable Hogue* (1970).

Slow motion, created by increasing the speed at which a subject is normally photographed, makes the action seem dream-like and fluid. As a technique, it is often employed to depict dreams and memories or to romanticize a subject or a setting. One of the concluding scenes of Arthur Penn's *Bonnie and Clyde* (1967), that in which Bonnie and Clyde are gunned down, is a widely acclaimed example of slow motion photography. In an interview, Penn explained that he used slow motion in that particular scene in order to impart a "balletic quality" to the film, to dramatize Bonnie and Clyde's "movement from life to myth."[5]

Thus, it should be clear that the way in which a story is told on film is at least as important as the story itself. Each of the factors that has been considered in this chapter—point of view, lenses, light, film stock, camera angle, and distance—are not mere technical embellishments. They are, in fact, the story itself.

REFERENCES

1. Alfred Kazin, ed., *Writers at Work: The Paris Review Interviews: Third Series* (New York: Viking Press, 1967), p. 264.

2. Arthur Knight, *The Liveliest Art* (New York: New American Library, 1957), p. 158.

3. For an excellent non-technical introduction to the art of cinematography, see Joseph Mascelli's *The Five C's of Cinematography* and Joseph Mercer's *An Introduction to Cinematography.*

4. Ralph Stephenson and J. R. Debrix, *The Cinema As Art* (Baltimore: Penguin Books, 1965), p. 172.

5. Joseph Gelmis, ed., *The Film Director As Superstar* (Garden City, N.Y.: Doubleday, 1970), p. 222.

Der Führer makes his entrance at the 1933 Nazi-party rally in Nuremburg. Flanking him, at one respectful pace to his rear, are Goering and Goebbels. Those are people lined up on either side of the corridor; they are cheering. This aerial shot is from Leni Riefenstahl's 1934 *Triumph of the Will.*

Courtesy of The Museum of Modern Art/Film Stills Archive

3

THE ART OF EDITING:

STRUCTURE

> One must learn to understand that editing is in actual fact a compulsory and deliberate guidance of the thoughts and associations of the spectator.
>
> V. I. PUDOVKIN[1]

Eisenstein's use of montage during the "Odessa Steps" sequence in *Potemkin* (1925) provides an important insight into the nature of the film experience: the use of time and space in film is very different from time and space as normally perceived.

Courtesy of The Museum of Modern Art/Film Stills Archive

At the turn of the century, the motion picture was evolving in two different directions: the documentary and the theatrical film. To the Lumière Brothers (this still is from their "Train Arriving in Station" [1895]), the motion picture camera represented a means to record and preserve the events of their time. To former magician Georges Méliès, however, the camera was an instrument that provided him the means to conjure and to create fantasies. Thus, from the Lumière Brothers arose the documentary tradition, from Méliès, the theatrical film.

Courtesy of The Museum of Modern Art/Film Stills Archive

Orson Welles' prolific use of unusual camera angles, as here in his 1942 *The Magnificent Ambersons*, is one of the trademarks of his flamboyant style in film making.

The Seventh Seal (1957) exemplifies the stark majesty of Ingmar Bergman's style. Here, the character Death makes his appearance beside a leaden sea.

Courtesy of Janus Films, Inc.

Reportedly, D. W. Griffith's complex and lavish spectacle *Intolerance* (1916) was shot without the benefit of a script.

Courtesy of The Museum of Modern Art/Film Stills Archive

Federico Fellini is today's most successful heir to the Surrealists of the 1920s and '30s. Here is a shot from his 1965 *Juliet of the Spirits*; it is interesting to note that in almost every one of his feature-length films there is a reference to the circus as a metaphor of life.

Courtesy of Audio Film Center/Ideal Pictures

Much of the humor of Chaplin's famous creation, *The Little Tramp,* is discoverable in the timing and rhythmic movements of the Tramp. Thus, though the external rhythms of Chaplin's films are usually fairly conventional, the internal rhythms of his films border on the sublime.

Courtesy of The Museum of Modern Art/Film Stills Archive

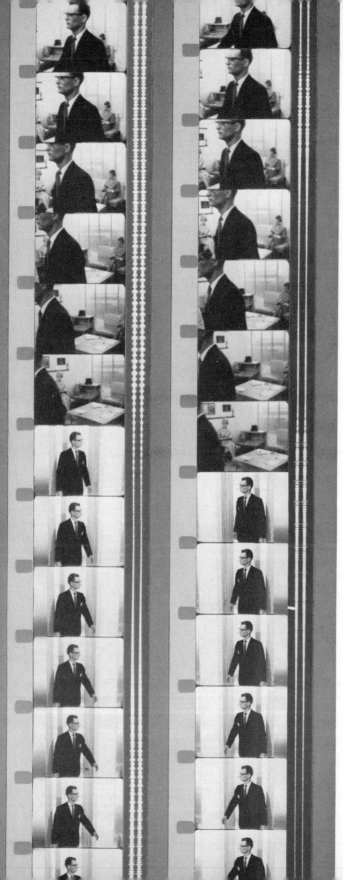

Note: In the film strips on these pages the sequence has been stepped up for the sake of clarity.

If a character walks out of the left-hand side of the frame, he should re-enter the next frame on the right side, for if he enters from the left, the audience is apt to assume that he has inexplicably turned around. Directors hire script girls to make sure of details like this for, in the complexity of the day-to-day shooting, they can be easily overlooked. See page 77.

Courtesy of Roundtable Films, Inc. From the film *Judging People*.

The same applies to a character who is talking to someone off-screen; he has to be facing his interlocutor.

Courtesy of Roundtable Films, Inc. From the film *Judging People*.

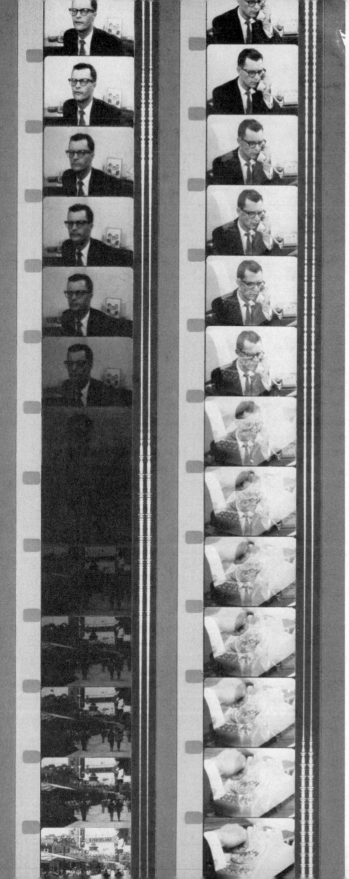

Left: an example of
fade-out and fade-in.

Right: an example
of a dissolve.

Courtesy of Roundtable Films, Inc.
From the film *Judging People*.

Left: an example of a wipe.

Right: an example of
split-screen montage.

Courtesy of Roundtable Films, Inc.
From the film *Judging People*.

R ARELY is the novelist or short-story writer thought of as an editor, a term usually applied to someone who supervises the production of a newspaper or periodical, or joins the various components of a film by the process of cutting, combining, and splicing. The word, however, is derived from the Latin word *ēdere*, which means *to bring forth* or *to publish*. Thus editing could be viewed as a process of selecting, arranging, and juxta-posing material in order to clarify or depict a subject in the most effective manner.

The problem that confronts the novelist, as well as the film maker, is to find the most dramatic method of revealing his subject. The selection of means is always bound up with the thematic nature of the story. A novelist, for example, might be deeply disturbed by the unscrupulous manner in which men often use each other for selfish ends. The general theme of man's inhumanity to man, however, is an enormous subject and could be illustrated in any number of ways: by examining war, by considering the callous social persecution of ethnic or racial minorities, by revealing the economic exploitation of the poor by the rich. A writer could conceivably attempt to examine all of these situations within the confines of a single novel, but there is a real possibility that depth would be sacrificed for scope. Perhaps the writer would decide to limit himself to only two of these possibilities. He thus initiates a process of selection.

Assume that he decides to consider the exploitation of the impoverished racial minorities by the more affluent. How is he to do it? Deciding that it would be impossible for him to deal adequately with all of the exploited minority groups in the world, he limits himself to the poor blacks of the inner-city ghettos. Since he is not interested in compiling a statistical abstract of the unbearable conditions in the black community, but wants to appeal to his reader's sense of compassion and justice, he ulti-mately decides to use a single family as representative of the entire community.

At each point in the development of this hypothetical novel, the writer has been faced with choices. In each instance, he has attempted to select what he considers to be the most dramatic and emotionally persuasive vehicle for his theme. Even though he has defined the scope of his subject, there still remains the problem of how best to reveal this particular family.

The writer decides that he does not want to deal with every aspect of the family's existence from birth to death, but only with those events that will best illuminate his theme. Thus, he decides to cover a time period of only one month. For the novelist, time is a malleable substance; he is not bound to observe its unfolding in a realistic manner. He might, for instance, open his novel by showing the family reduced to abject poverty and despair, and use subsequent chapters to show how their plight came about. Thus, time is inverted for dramatic purposes. The reader's foreknowledge of the family's fate will certainly affect his response to the story. For example, if the family should enjoy a brief respite from its bleak existence—an apparent change of fortune or a happy moment—the reader will view the incident in a somewhat ironic light.

In the course of writing the novel, the author will also consider ways to heighten the drama of the family's predicament, such as juxtaposition or parallel action. A diamond is a beautiful stone in nearly any circumstances, but placed next to a common pebble the exquisite beauty of the diamond is heightened. In the same manner, juxtaposing the meagerness of the black family's dinner with the comparative lavishness of the typical white, middle-class family's meal dramatically emphasizes the discrepancies in the two life-styles.

Parallel action, on the other hand, usually deals with two different but related actions that are occurring simultaneously. The novelist might include a scene which shows the father of the black family being turned down for a construction job "because there are no openings at present"; while at the same time, in another part of the city, a construction foreman is calling the office for additional men because he is so shorthanded that he is behind on the job.

Thus, even though the writer is not usually thought of as an editor, he must in fact make a series of decisions that are editorial in nature. The main distinction between the novelist and the film maker as editors lies in the nature of their mediums. The writer deals with words. He assembles his words in a manner (style) that is appropriate to his subject. Obviously, a flippant style would be totally inappropriate to the struggles of the black

family. Through his choice of words and in his description, the
writer attempts to convey his theme, and if he has been successful in his choices, the finished novel will be emotionally persuasive—it will move the reader.

The starting point for a film maker is usually his script,
although sometimes there are exceptions. D. W. Griffith's lavish
and complex *Intolerance,* for example, was reportedly shot without benefit of a script. And Jean-Luc Godard has been known to
have actors and technicians sitting around the set waiting for him
to decide what they will do next. But most directors use a script
like a blueprint for the film: it helps them predict not only what
they will need in the way of time, personnel, and materials to
produce the film, but also what kinds of artistic and technical
problems will be involved. Alfred Hitchcock, for instance, is so
meticulous in his preparation of a script that French director
Jacques Becker considers him "the director who gets the least
surprised when he looks at the rushes."[2]

The film script should be looked on as a kind of guide to the
film; it is not, of course, the film itself, any more than a map is
an actual territory. On the other hand, the script is not quite as
rigid a document as a map or blueprint; the film maker can make
changes in the script as he proceeds, but the builder who ignores
the architect's specifications may well find the building tumbling
down upon his head.

Most commercial scripts go through four major stages: the
synopsis or outline, the treatment, the screenplay, and the shooting script. The *outline* states the complete story but does not go
into detail (it may, for instance, be as brief as three paragraphs).
The *treatment,* on the other hand, resembles something between
a novel and a stage play. Though it may contain some narration,
it usually supplies all the intended dialogue and describes the
film's basic or key scenes (a treatment for a full-length motion
picture is generally 30 to 200 pages in length). The *screenplay*
refines the treatment even further by eliminating any narrative
passages and supplying the remainder of the missing scenes. It is
at this point that the script is checked for unity, balance, variety,
tension, comic relief (if necessary), or any other organizational
problems. The *shooting script,* which is primarily the responsibility of the director, includes all the technical descriptions that
the cameraman, set designer, musical director, prop man, and

editor will need in order to do their jobs. At this point, the script can still be revised if it appears the completed film will run overly long, if the actors discover that a certain scene doesn't play well, or if budget and production pressures necessitate the elimination of some scenes.

The actual raw materials of the film maker, however, are strips of film containing images which, in combination, will ultimately comprise the finished film. The film maker is always faced with the problem of finding a concrete image to convey his meaning. A novelist could write that a character "sensed a latent danger in even commonplace events," but the film maker would have to *show* commonplace events as seen through the eyes of a tremendously frightened man. Crossing the street would be revealed as a harrowing experience, strangers would be seen as potential assailants, and innocent acts and gestures perceived as threatening.

The Russian film maker and theoretician, V. I. Pudovkin, writes in *Film Technique* that "the foundation of film art is *editing*."[3] Later in the same work, he attempts to explain why the editorial process is so critical to the film experience:

> [I]t appears that the active raw material [of the film director] is no other than those *pieces of celluloid* on which, from various view-points, the separate movements of the action have been shot. From nothing but these pieces is created those appearances upon the screen that form the filmic representation of the action shot. And thus the material of the film director consists not of real processes happening in real space and real time, but those pieces of celluloid on which these processes have been recorded. This celluloid is entirely subject to the will of the director who edits it.[4]

Thus, it is extremely important to realize that the "reality" of a film derives far more from the selection, arrangement, and juxtaposition of these pieces of celluloid than from the mere reproduction of images that exist in the external world. In other words, film is capable of creating its own reality, one that may have no counterpart in the "real" world.

For obvious (i.e., financial) reasons, a film is rarely shot in sequence. In a studio, there may be a set for a particular scene that is used, according to the script, at the beginning and again at the end of the film. It would be absurd to film the early scene, tear down the set, and then reconstruct it at a later date; so the concluding scene will be shot out of sequence. The same holds true for a film that makes use of different locales. Every scene or sequence that takes place in a given locale will be finished there before the company moves on to a new location. This means that both cameraman and actor must work in a piecemeal fashion, while in the theater actors and technicians can experience a sense of emotional continuity. Sometimes only the director and the script writer are aware of how the completed film will appear to the audience. Occasionally, as in the case of Fellini's 8½ (1963), only the director knows; and sometimes not even he, as in John Huston's largely improvised *Beat the Devil* (1954).

The completed film, then, is usually six to eight reels (the standard length of a reel is 900 to 1200 feet) of exposed film that will ultimately comprise the 90 to 120 minutes (approximately) that the audience views on the screen. As a process, editing usually goes through several stages. The director, while he is in the process of filming the action, could decide on the set that there are several takes (the shots recorded during the production) he knows he doesn't want; an actor could have muffed a line, been temporarily out of character, sneezed, or perhaps a technician wandered onto the set by accident. Those pieces of exposed film will never be processed. Thus, the editing process begins even before the film goes to the cutting room. Once the film does reach the cutting room, the editor puts together the "first draft" of the film, known as the *rough cut*. In the rough cut, the editor selects the best of the takes and joins them together according to the order established by the script. At this point, the film maker confers with the editor to refine the rough cut into the most effective film version, known as the *fine cut*. Lastly, the supportive material—dialogue, sound, music—is selected and combined in the desired order (this process is referred to as the *mix*) and recorded on the film's sound track. This brief, superficial description of the editing process, however, does not begin to suggest the complexity, the countless decisions and vast amounts of time that go into the editing of a film. There are numerous examples of films shot in a couple of weeks that were over a year or more in the editing process. Leni Reifenstahl's film *Olympia*, for example, described only the events of the 1936 Olympic Games, but it was over a year and a half in editing.[5]

One cannot exaggerate the importance of editing to the development of the film as an art form. By and large, the technical advances that refined and facilitated the editorial process were responsible for liberating the film from its dependence on traditional theatrical conventions. A very brief examination of some of the high points of the development of editing can suggest how the film changed from an interesting experiment to an art form.

Viewed historically,[6] the development of film as an art emerges as a direct consequence of its movement away from theatrical conventions. Many turn-of-the-century films—those of the Lumière Brothers, for example—were simply unadorned shots of interesting events (see p. 58); the camera was placed in position, turned on, and subsequently recorded whatever passed in front of its lens. This particular style assumed that the camera was a passive witness to events, that it was the events themselves that provided whatever interest the film would contain. In fact, the only distinguishable difference between this employment of the motion picture camera and the still camera was that the film moved. And, in almost every instance, these early films centered around a single incident.

A short time later, film makers began attempting stories. The films tended to be longer, they did make use of continuity of subject matter, but each scene was distinctly a separate event. In 1902, Thomas Edison's cameraman, Edwin S. Porter, created a short film entitled *The Life of an American Fireman.*[7] Porter's film was unique in two respects: first, it made use of previously existing film footage; second, Porter managed to suggest the illusion of continuity of action between separate scenes. The audience, for example, sees an exterior shot of a burning building, and watches as the firemen arrive; the film then dissolves to an interior shot of the building showing a mother and child overcome by smoke; the door opens, the fireman enters and carries out the stricken mother. Next, the film dissolves to the exterior of the building to show the mother pleading with the fireman to re-enter the building to save her child. The audience watches while the fireman goes into the building and, after a few moments, comes out with the child cradled in his arms. Porter's use of existing material suggested that the "reality" of the film experience was derived not so much from the action photographed, but from the joining together of the strips of celluloid. In viewing the film.

the audience was not able to tell the difference between the already-existing footage and the footage that had been shot expressly for the film. Thus, Porter demonstrated that if illusion of continuity could be achieved by the skillful juxtaposition of shots, the audience would accept the transitions as credible.

Despite Porter's important contributions, the camera still remained anchored to its fixed position. In the next few years, however, some significant changes took place in film narration. By 1915, D. W. Griffith, in his *Birth of a Nation*, was making use of numerous technical innovations. The camera moved from wide panoramic shots to close-ups; areas of the screen image were selectively darkened (masked) for dramatic emphasis; the screen was sometimes divided into two separate but related images; the overall action was fragmented into components (long shots, close-ups, etc.) and the finished scene reconstructed from these components; and the timing of shots was employed for dramatic purposes. This last development involved both rapid cutting, to suggest the exhilaration of a chase, and juxtaposing events taking place at the same time, to increase the tension. For example, near the end of the film the audience sees some members of the Cameron family trapped in a log cabin fighting off a mob of Union soldiers, while the next shot shows the Ku Klux Klan racing to their rescue. By cutting back and forth between these two actions, Griffith intensifies audience excitement considerably; early viewers were probably on the edge of their seats, wondering if the rescuers would make it in time.

By Griffith's day, the film had made several radical departures from the conventions of the stage. The use of the close-up not only increased the film maker's control over his audience's response, but it also gave rise to a new style of acting that was much more restrained than the acting style of the theater. The fragmentation of a scene introduced an unprecedented depiction of reality. The timing of the length of a shot made it possible for the film maker to influence his viewers' emotional reaction to a given scene. Movement of the camera exchanged the artificial frontal perspective of the theater for a more realistic shifting perspective.

By 1925, Russian film makers such as Sergei Eisenstein and V. I. Pudovkin had developed the technique of *montage*.[8] Montage is a process of creative editing whereby the images derive their meaning from juxtaposition with other images. Eisenstein, for example, explained that the continuity of a film should be created by a series of shocks and conflicts, and that it is the splicing of images that produces the conflict. Montage has also been employed to compress time. For example, rather than showing a man emerge from a cab, walk to the door of a building, enter the lobby, press the elevator button, wait, enter the elevator, ascend to the fifth floor, enter the hall, and proceed to his office, the film maker need only show the man leaving the cab, then cut to him entering the building, and finally cut to him pushing open the door to his office. The audience watching this latter sequence will assume that the actor has gone through all the intervening steps even though they haven't actually witnessed them. Montage can also be used to produce the opposite effect—the expansion of time.

In the famous "Odessa Steps" sequence in *The Battleship Potemkin* (1926), Eisenstein shows a force of Cossacks marching down the steps slaughtering the citizens of Odessa who have gathered there (see p. 58). By constantly moving back and forth from the descent of the Cossacks to the reactions of the stricken and terrified people, Eisenstein actually elongates time. In other words, the running time of the segment is much longer than it would actually take the Cossacks to descend the steps.

This particular use of montage provides an important insight into the nature of the film experience: the use of time and space in film is very different from time and space as normally perceived. Eisenstein's purpose is not to depict the actual passage of time realistically, but to portray it dramatically. By elongating time, he has succeeded in heightening the drama of the incident. This is simply another way of saying that events vary in dramatic intensity, and it makes sense to devote more film time to dramatically important events and less to insignificant ones.

A hypothetical example might serve to clarify how a film maker manipulates time. A man arises, brushes his teeth, eats breakfast while reading the newspaper, and exchanges a few words of conversation with his wife. He dresses, leaves his home, and walks to the street corner. The bus arrives and he boards it. The driver is surly because the man does not have the right amount of change. The man rides to work reading the newspaper. He leaves the bus and walks a block to his office. Upon entering the building, he boards the elevator and, after a few moments, disembarks and walks to his office. As he enters the office, he says hello to the secretaries and then proceeds to his desk; he hears muffled laughter behind him. Seated at his desk, he begins to work on the papers piled up before him. He drops one of the papers, bends down to pick it up and notices that, in his hurry to leave home in the morning, he had put on two different shoes. He experiences embarrassment. The remainder of the morning, he works at his desk. Still feeling embarrassed about the shoes, he remains at his desk through the lunch hour. His stomach begins to growl. Later in the afternoon, he is called into the manager's office and chewed out because of a miscalculation in one of the papers he had handled. Humiliated, he takes the paper and returns to his desk, whereupon he discovers that the error is not his. He calls the guilty party to his desk. The other person, unperturbed by the incident, shrugs it off by saying, "Well, everyone makes mistakes," and promptly returns to his desk. Five o'clock, and the man leaves the office, retracing the route he had taken that morning. He arrives at the bus stop just in time to see his bus, a few seconds early, pulling away from the curb. It begins to drizzle and he has to wait twenty minutes in the rain. After he arrives home, his wife casually asks him if he had remembered to pay the light bill while he was in town, and the man explodes in fury.

Obviously, this example includes too many superfluities. It is unlikely that an audience would be interested in the man brushing his teeth, eating breakfast, riding the bus, walking to work, handling the papers, and returning home. The audience "knows" all this already; consequently, the film maker can eliminate these events as being dramatically unimportant. What is important about the scene is the series of frustrating events that ultimately produce the angry explosion. These incidents make the man's outburst credible.

The film maker could probably concentrate on the frustrating incidents in five minutes of film time. Since the audience is fully prepared for the scene that takes place when the man arrives home, it would be legitimate for the film maker to elongate this incident, the natural culmination of his dramatic buildup; it is more important than the minor dramatic incidents that precede it. In this example, time serves a dramatic rather than a realistic master.

Film is capable of altering not only time but space as well. V. I. Pudovkin, in his *Film Technique*, pointed out that Eisenstein's "Odessa Steps" episode was shot in three different geographical locations.[9] The battleship was filmed at Odessa, but the stone lions which appear in this scene are located in the Crimea, and the iron gates are in Moscow. Thus the location that appears in this scene does not exist in actuality. By the relatively simple act of joining strips of film, the film maker is capable of creating virtually any kind of spatial relationship that he desires.

The film maker could, for example, show the audience a frontal view of a rustic mountain cabin in the Smokies. The viewer would see the mountain scene flanking the cabin. Inside the cabin, the camera shows the occupant walking toward a window in the rear of the cabin. The camera, in close-up, shows the occupant looking out of the window. The audience sees what he sees—the Sahara Desert! The example, of course, is farfetched, but it does point up what the film maker can achieve with locale. He is not bound to mechanically reproduce reality as he finds it, but he rarely alters time and space without a valid reason—the changes he introduces will always be related to meaning.

Another aspect of the editing process that is intimately related to meaning is the *rhythm* of a film. Life is filled with rhythmical patterns: the very act of breathing, the beating of the heart, the passage of a day, the changing of the seasons, the rotation of the earth. It is also clear that rhythm is related to meaning: a rapid increase in breathing is usually related to excitement, a rise in the rate of the heartbeat may be prompted by anxiety and fear. Although few students of poetry would fail to consider the relation of rhythm to meaning in a poem, many students of film overlook the contribution that rhythm can make to a film.

Basically, a film deals with two kinds of rhythm: *internal rhythm*, which is conveyed within the shot itself (a shot of a man strolling would create a slow internal rhythm, whereas if the same man broke into a run it would increase the tempo); and *external rhythm*, which is the actual length of time a given shot remains on the screen (a series of very brief one-second shots would impart a fast external rhythm to a scene, whereas shots that ran a couple of minutes in length would generate a slow external rhythm). Rhythm, like everything that the film maker does, supports and intensifies meaning.

In many ways, the rhythm of a scene corresponds to the way in which an observer would ordinarily perceive that scene. If a person were standing in a room watching four men seated at a table playing cards, the scene would probably move relatively slowly. The eyes of the observer would blink at normal rhythm; the action would shift slowly from one player to another. However, if the game were to erupt into a brawl, there would be a simultaneous increase of tempo and movement. The film maker would attempt to approximate the responses of the observer by decreasing the length of the cuts. The shift from the slow-moving cuts of the card playing to the rapid chaotic cuts of the fight would approximate the viewer's reaction to such a scene.

On the other hand, to employ quick cuts in a scene that is generally quiet and peaceful would be very inappropriate, because the rapidity of the cuts would fight the emotional content of the scene. This is not to suggest that every quiet scene will employ "slow" cuts and every exciting scene "fast" cuts. What does determine the pace of the scene is the emotional effect that the film maker is trying to evoke. For example, the curling of smoke is generally a slow, languorous, lazy movement, but if the film maker is trying to suggest that various chemical elements that smoke throws into our atmosphere are polluting our environment at an alarming rate, he would want to visually modify the normal depiction of rising smoke. He might show a quick cut of smoke billowing out of a car's exhaust, cut to a truck's exhaust, to a jet plane, to an incinerator, and finally, to a slow-burning garbage dump. If the film maker cuts from shot to shot quickly enough, the viewer not only receives the impression that the pollution is spreading at an alarming rate, but also senses, because of the very speed at which the images are moving, that the whole problem of pollution has somehow gotten out of control. In other words, through the use of accelerated external rhythm and juxtaposition, the film maker is able to create concepts that represent more than the sum of the original materials.

An inventive example of this particular technique is found in Charles Braverman's three-minute *American Time Capsule* (many television viewers first saw this film on the now-defunct "Smothers Brothers Comedy Hour"). In essence, the film is a series of still photos, chronologically arranged, depicting the history of the United States. The images, which are synchronized with the song "Beat That Drum," flash on the screen at a dizzying rate of speed, and when the beginning of the twentieth century is reached, the rate of speed is accelerated even more. This increase implies that the pace of life became almost unbearably hectic at this point in our history—an inference based solely on the film's external rhythm, as the still photos, obviously, possess no internal rhythm.

In the pollution example, a rapid external technique was imposed upon material with a basically slow internal rhythm in order to make a serious point. The very same technique can also be utilized to create comic or satiric effects. It could be argued, for example, that everything possesses its own particular rhythm, including various activities: people walk in a recognizable rhythm, plants grow in certain rhythms. To alter the normal rhythm of an activity is literally to force a viewer to perceive its meaning differently. Baking a cake, for example, is ordinarily a slow, methodical process. However, if the film maker were to impose a rapid external rhythm on the activities taking place in the kitchen, the baking process would take on an absurd, frantic, and nonsensical dimension. If the film maker wished to exaggerate this effect even more, he might decide to film the action in fast motion, in which case he would be combining a rapid internal rhythm with a fast external rhythm. The award-winning television show *Laugh-In* based many of its sight gags on just this type of technique. Similarly, in novels and plays, comic exchanges are usually characterized by brevity and a corresponding increase in tempo.

External rhythm is a largely mechanical effect, created by the duration of a shot, whereas internal rhythm is more natural, arising from within the scene itself. In cutting a film, however, the film maker must consider many other factors as well. The cuts, except where the film maker is trying to produce an unusual effect, should proceed naturally and intelligibly. If a character who is standing to the left of a frame looking toward the left should speak to another character out-of-frame, the audience naturally looks for the other character's response. The other character will probably be shown, in the following shot, standing to the right of the frame, looking right, toward the character who has just spoken. If he were shown in the same position as the first speaker, the two shots would be very confusing. Likewise, if a character walks out of the left-hand side of the frame, he should reenter the next frame on the right side, for if he enters from the left the audience is apt to assume that he has inexplicably turned around.

The film maker should anticipate the audience's response to a shot, and, in most instances, fulfill its expectations. For example, if the film maker shows two characters walking down the street engrossed in a lively conversation, then cuts to a close-up of an open manhole, the audience will begin to anticipate one of the men falling in. This does not mean that the film maker must have one of the characters fall in, for he could just as easily have a worker rise up in the manhole at just the right moment to provide a stepping stone. The point is that he has to make *some* use of the manhole.

By the same token, his shots should be intelligible to the audience. If the film maker shows a billboard or a letter, there should be enough time for the audience to read it. In general, the audience should have more time to comprehend a long shot than a close-up, for the long shot takes more time to perceive. The audience should also know where a scene is taking place; an arbitrary shift from one location to another with no preparation is unnecessarily disorienting. Along the same lines, an audience will need more time to comprehend the new location, object, or character.

Also, whenever perspective or camera position is altered in a film there should be a reason for the change. That is, when we see a long shot of a man reading a note, the following shot is likely to be a close-up showing us what he is reading. To cut from a long shot of a man in profile to a frontal long shot of the same man just for the sake of a different image makes little sense. If, on the other hand, the frontal long shot revealed that there was someone standing behind the man, observing him, the audience would learn something from the altered perspective and the shot would be a valid one.

The cut is simply one way of moving from one image to another. In general, the use of a cut in a film suggests that there has been no break in the action, that the movement of the scene is continuous. There are, to be sure, a number of different ways that a film maker is able to cut from one shot to another. He can, for example, cut from one shape to another, similar shape, as Stanley Kubrick did in his *2001: A Space Odyssey* when he dramatically cut from the shot of the femur bone spiraling up into the sky to the shot of the pencil-shaped spacecraft orbiting the moon. He can also cut on movement, as in *The Graduate*, when Mike Nichols cuts from the shot of Benjamin diving into the pool to the shot of him landing in bed with Mrs. Robinson.

Next to the common cut, the most frequently used cuts are the "cross cut" and "cutaway." The cross cut has sometimes been described as the "meanwhile, back at the ranch" cut. In other words, the film maker cuts back and forth between actions occurring simultaneously but in two different geographical locations (e.g., the reinforcements discover that an avalanche has closed the pass and they'll have to take the long way around; fifty miles away the defenders of the fort are running out of ammunition). Another variation on the cross cut is when the film maker cuts from one historical period to another (for example, cutting from a shot of Herbert Hoover delivering a presidential campaign speech to a similar shot of John Kennedy doing the same). The cutaway, on the other hand, occurs when the film maker cuts to a shot which reveals a portion of the action that was *not shown* in the previous shot (for instance, cutting from a tight shot of two young boys fist-fighting to a shot of one boy's mother pushing through the crowd around them shouting, "What's going on here?"). There are, of course, other ways of providing transitions between shots and scenes. Many of these techniques are introduced during the editing process.

The *fade* (see p. 64) was once a rather common transitional device in film making. Basically, there are two different kinds: the *fade-in*, in which the viewer sees a totally black screen, then watches the screen gradually lighten to reveal an image; and the *fade-out*, in which the viewer observes the lighted image darken to a black screen. Because the fade is of longer duration than the cut, it has the effect of breaking the flow of action, separating, as it were, one scene from the next. Consequently, the fade not only retards time, but also gives the audience an opportunity to momentarily consider the preceding scene.

The *dissolve*, like the fade, does not enjoy the popularity it once did, but it is still used occasionally as a transitional device. A dissolve gradually merges two different images. For example, the audience might be looking at the skyline of New York, then gradually become aware of yet another image, a view of Paris, behind the New York skyline. The New York skyline disappears, leaving only the Parisian scene. The implication is that the scene of action has shifted from New York to Paris. The dissolve is sometimes used in films to introduce and terminate flashback sequences.

The *super* or *superimposure* is very close to the dissolve, the only difference being that both shots are held on the screen simultaneously. What happens is that two shots are printed on top of each other so that when they are projected on the screen, the viewer sees both of them at the same time. The super has the effect of suggesting that two separate but related actions are occurring at the same time. By showing an audience an image of a burning building superimposed on an image of a fire truck racing to the rescue, the film maker indicates that both activities are happening simultaneously.

Another technique that has lately come into fashion to indicate simultaneous action is *split-screen montage*. In this instance, the screen is divided up into separate areas. Each area of the screen shows a separate but related activity. For example, it is conceivable that a fire scene could be handled by this technique. The film maker could split the screen into five areas. In one section, he could show the exterior of the burning building; in another, a woman trapped inside the building being overcome by smoke; in another section, a man poised in one of the windows of the building working up enough courage to jump; a fourth section could show firemen smashing in the door of the building with axes, while the fifth might show the fire chief, on his two-way radio, calling for additional assistance.

Two other transitional techniques, rarely used today, are the *flip* and the *wipe*. (The flip is still used fairly extensively in TV, a medium which, through the economic challenge it poses, has freed today's film from many of its former restrictions and taboos.) In the wipe, the viewer witnesses one shot changing to another by means of a moving line which usually travels from side to side or top to bottom of the frame. As the line moves across the image, it simultaneously "wipes out" the old image and reveals the new one. The flip is a slight modification of the wipe, for the image appears to roll over, revealing another image; typically, the rotation is on either a vertical or horizontal axis.

At present, most film makers tend to avoid the flip and the wipe; the consensus of feeling seems to be that the cut, fade, and dissolve provide more "natural" visual transitions than the flip or the wipe. Today, indeed, the cut has become the paramount transitional device.

It is also rare to see a contemporary film maker employing the *mask* (François Truffaut is an exception here), although it was a favorite device of D. W. Griffith's. Basically, the mask darkens selected areas of the image in order to produce a special visual effect. Using the mask, the film maker can make a shot appear as it would through binoculars, a periscope, or a keyhole. Griffith, for instance, used a device called the "iris" whereby he would darken the frame except for a small circular area in the center; he would then "open up" the iris to reveal the entire scene. Because the iris technique is identified almost exclusively with the early silent film, some modern directors have used it in historical films to convey a sense of time past. François Truffaut, for example, employed the iris in his *Wild Child* (1970), a film that was set in the late nineteenth century.

Although film makers use nearly all the editorial techniques mentioned above, their films tend to be remarkably different experiences. After witnessing only a few minutes of a Welles, a Bergman, and a Fellini film, the viewer would be acutely aware that he was dealing with three quite different sensibilities. This awareness proceeds from the recognition of readily distinguishable differences in the three films: differences in subject matter, differences in approach and, particularly, differences in the presentation of visual images. Style, of course, is not merely a technique that is arbitrarily imposed upon the material, but rather a method that is indigenous to the story.

An essential element in the overall visual style of any film is the type of editing style it employs. Even though individual editing styles may be as unique as their creators, it is possible to distinguish between two very general stylistic approaches: *continuity editing* and *dynamic editing*.

In general, continuity editing attempts to portray the action of a story in a "realistic" manner, that is, the emphasis is on the creation of a smooth, continuous flow of events. In many respects, this technique could be likened to the experience of the theater, for the depiction of the story (its movement and dialogue) tends to proceed in a predictable, continuous line. This style of editing will generally make use of long, uninterrupted stretches of action, and is likely to involve cutting on movement between shots. For example, if the film maker were attempting to film the traditional chase scene of the western by means of continuity editing, he would, in all probability, remain with only one of the two parties. The audience would tend to identify with the heroes; consequently, the film maker would reveal the chase from their point of view. If the pursued are the heroes, their vantage point would be used. Although it might seem that this technique would result in a static chase, this is not always the case; in *Butch Cassidy and the Sundance Kid*, director George Roy Hill uses it with great dramatic effect. Paul Newman and Robert Redford undergo a number of increasingly difficult ordeals in order to "shake off" a posse that is after them, dead or alive. They use every trick in the book to throw their nameless, relentless pursuers off their track . . . to no avail. Newman's despairing wail, "Who *are* those guys?" provides one of the serio-comic highlights of the 1970 film season.

A more conventional way of depicting the chase sequence, though, is by means of dynamic editing. In this instance, the viewer would see a medium shot of the heroes galloping across the plains and immediately afterward, another medium shot of the villains in pursuit. Dynamic editing disregards "realistic" spatial relationships in order to concentrate on the drama of the chase; it is clear that the juxtaposition of the two medium shots of the heroes and the villains has no counterpart in reality.

Dynamic editing usually proceeds by the technique of fragmenting the story into carefully selected pieces of action. In this style of editing, the emphasis shifts to relational contrasts, which may give rise to responses that are more in the eye of the beholder than in the film itself. In an experiment, Russian director V. I. Pudovkin and film theoretician L. V. Kuleshov[10] recorded some footage of an actor with a completely neutral expression. They then cut up this footage and interspersed it with shots of a bowl of soup, a coffin containing a woman, and a young girl playing with a toy. When the film was projected, the audience was impressed by the actor's subtle acting style. They "saw" him expressing longing at the bowl of soup, grief at the loss of the woman, and joy when he perceived the young girl at play.

Clearly, it was the juxtaposition of the shots, rather than their inherent value, that created the meaning.

The entire philosophy of montage developed by Eisenstein and Pudovkin is very much in accord with the principles of dynamic editing, and it could certainly be argued that the introduction of dynamic editing was one of the main factors in freeing the film from the slavish imitation of theatrical techniques. Today, it is rare to see a film maker create an entire film which is exclusively devoted to one of these editing styles; more typically, the two styles are used in combination to help create a logical rhythm for the film as a whole.

One might wonder how, if most film makers use both continuity and dynamic editing, an individual directing style is achieved. Ultimately, the style of the individual film maker is determined by virtually every aspect of the film. It was suggested earlier that the subject matter of the film must be considered. The viewer must evaluate what landscape the film maker has decided to explore: the relationships that exist between individuals, the effect of society upon the individual or a larger canvas—perhaps the sweeping events of a historical period. Obviously, the choice of social, historical, and physical landscapes determines to a great extent how the story will be handled. What kind of attitude does the film maker take toward his material? Is he objective, scornful, sardonic, satiric, bemused, reverent, remorseful? More importantly, how does he realize the story? Does he work in black and white or in color? Does his use of either medium possess special characteristics? Is the visual texture rich, garish, grainy, dull, or bright? How are the shots and scenes presented? Are they cluttered and busy, or are they stark and motionless? What kinds of angles, lenses, and editing techniques are employed? What contribution does the sound make? How fast or slow do the images move? Who are the characters, and how are they revealed by the actors? It might appear that these questions are directed toward what the film is about, but what the film is *about* is an abstraction. It could be *about* man's inhumanity to man, *about* love, *about* injustice; what it's about is not necessarily what it *means,* however. If you comprehend the style of the film, you will simultaneously grasp its meaning; for the style is the medium that conveys the meaning.

Thus far, the elements and techniques of editing have been dealt with out of context. At this point, it might be useful to examine a portion of a hypothetical script, involving a single scene, and so demonstrate how the editor goes about selecting material; why he selects what he does; and how the joining of these strips of celluloid affects the response of the viewer.

The scene outlined below describes a fugitive who goes to a public park to meet a "friend." The friend, however, has informed the police of the forthcoming meeting and the park has been staked out. Dialogue and sound have been eliminated in order to concentrate on the impact of the visuals. The numbers to the right of the shot description indicate in seconds the running time of each shot (approximately one and one-half feet of film are projected every second).

E.L.S./extreme long shot; L.S./long shot; M.L.S./medium long shot; M.S./medium shot; M.C.U./medium close-up; C.U./close-up; E.C.U./extreme close-up.

Shot description	Running time of shot in seconds
1. M.S. of fugitive in an apartment, standing before a mirror, buckling on a shoulder holster. He looks to the left. cut to [all transitions between shots are cuts unless otherwise indicated]:	20
2. C.U. Clock on the table: three-thirty.	2
3. M.S. Fugitive walks to door of apartment and opens door into the hall.	10
4. M.S. Door of a bus opening inward and fugitive boarding bus. He deposits fare and moves toward the back of the bus.	20
5. M.C.U. Fugitive seated beside an older woman dressed in black. Buildings, store fronts, pedestrians, etc., are visible through the windows of the bus. The bus moves from right to left.	30

Shot description	Running time of shot in seconds
6. L.S. Reverse Angle [i.e., the viewer sees this scene from the opposite angle of previous shot]. Group of people standing on corner. Bus comes into frame from left side and discharges passengers. Fugitive gets off. Park can be seen in the background.	15
7. M.S. Fugitive at entrance of the park purchasing newspaper from a vendor.	10
8. M.C.U. Fugitive seated at park bench reading paper. Looks at wristwatch.	5
9. E.C.U. Wristwatch: four o'clock.	3
10. M.S. Fugitive lighting a cigarette as he continues to read the paper.	10
11. C.U. Paper on the ground beside the park bench.	3
12. M.S. Fugitive dropping cigarette on ground and grinding it out with his foot. Looks in the direction of the park entrance.	10
13. L.S. Park entrance. Couple walks in holding hands.	10

Dissolve to:

14. C.U. Fugitive's foot grinding out another cigarette. There is the litter of a half-dozen cigarettes lying on the ground.	8
15. L.S. Man rising and beginning to pace back and forth in front of the park bench.	20
16. C.U. Park pigeon pacing nervously.	10
17. M.S. Fugitive sitting down again; looks at watch.	12
18. E.C.U. Wristwatch: five o'clock.	3

Shot description

19. L.S. Park entrance—light beginning to
    fail—couple with their arms around each
    other departing.   15

20. M.S. Fugitive seated at park bench. Picks
    up discarded paper.   10

21. C.U. Newspaper; page is open to a
    travel ad.   8

Dissolve to:

22. M.S. (High contrast) Fugitive dressed in
    expensive clothes; he stands on the balcony
    of what looks to be a lavish hotel. The
    door opens behind him and an attractive
    woman, carrying a drink on a tray, appears.
    She places the tray on a table. He puts a
    cigarette to his lips. She deliberately
    picks up a lighter, lights it, and
    begins to bring the light toward
    his cigarette.   25

Dissolve to:

23. M.S. Fugitive back on park bench, cigarette
    dangling from mouth. Hand comes into frame
    holding a light.   8

24. C.U. Fugitive's face; look of surprise and
    fear, followed by recognition.   5

25. C.U. of man who lit cigarette. His face is
    tense and his eyes slowly shift right.   7

26. C.U. of fugitive turning his eyes in the
    same direction.   6

27. L.S. Large bush near park entrance; man
    standing behind the bush.   5

28. C.U. Same shot as #25. Man's eyes
    shift left.   6

29. L.S. Man, dressed in conservative business
    suit, sitting on a park bench reading
    a newspaper.   5

| | Running time of shot in seconds |
| Shot description | |

30. Same shot as #25. Man's eyes look upward.   6

31. E.L.S. Roof of a building facing park. A
    figure is seen silhouetted against the sky.   8

32. M.S. Fugitive jumps up and rushes from
    bench; camera pans with him as he runs into
    the bushes.   5

33. L.S. Man on park bench drops newspaper,
    jumps up while pulling out a pistol,
    and begins to run toward the camera.   7

34. L.S. Man runs out from behind bush near
    park entrance. He holds a gun in his hand
    and runs toward the camera.   6

35. E.L.S. Figure on rooftop raises small
    radio to his lips.   8

36. M.S. Police switchboard operator seen
    talking and pushing plugs into switchboard.   6

37. L.S. Police squad car driving away from
    camera, stops abruptly, turns around and
    heads back in the direction of the camera.   10

38. Super M.S. of motorcycle cop starting his
    cycle. C.U. of interior of squad car, one
    officer talking on two-way radio.   5

39. M.S. Fugitive running through bushes.   6

40. M.S. Plainclothes detective running
    through bushes.   4

41. M.L.S. Motorcycle cop approaching park.   3

42. L.S. Squad car coming to an abrupt stop at
    another corner of the park.   2

43. E.C.U. Fugitive, now breathing heavily,
    still running.   5

This scene, or some variation on it, has been seen countless times on the screen; it represents a basic ingredient of the typical "cops and robbers" film. Originality aside, it does serve to illustrate most of the basic elements of the editing process.

First, notice what has happened to time. The events described here took, in "real" time, about two and one-half hours to occur, but the screen version lasts about four and one-half minutes. Thus, two and one-half hours are squeezed into less than five minutes. The film maker is able to do this by eliminating what is unessential to his purpose. Rather than giving the viewer a detailed transcription of all the events, he merely sketches in the outlines of the action. For example, the cut from shot #3 to shot #4 eliminates not only the fugitive's journey from his apartment to the bus stop but also his wait at the stop. The shots, however, are connected by means of camera distances (they are both medium shots) and the connected movements of the apartment door and door of the bus. Likewise, shot #14 suggests the passage of time by showing the accumulation of cigarette butts on the ground. In a more obvious fashion, the close-ups of the clock and the wristwatch accomplish the same purpose. They are not arbitrary shots, though, for they indicate the fugitive's nervousness and impatience.

A quick glance at the time allotted to each shot will indicate that the time a shot is permitted to remain on the screen is directly related to the pace of the action. The early parts of the scene describe a slow internal movement; consequently, the duration of the shots is longer. But, in the latter part of the scene, the internal movement accelerates during the chase, and the briefer shots emphasize that excitement.

Some of the shots also provide the viewer with certain visual clues as to the forthcoming events. When the fugitive is on the bus in shot #5, a certain ominousness is created by having him seated next to the widow dressed in black. In the park (shot #16), the script makes use of a film simile that not only parodies the fugitive's movements (the nervous jerky movements of the pigeon are analogous to the fugitive's pacing), but also comments upon his plight—having been set up by the informer, he is, literally, a "sitting duck."

Most of the transitions used in this scene are cuts. Their use suggests that the action is continuous. In three instances, however, the script calls for dissolves. The first dissolve, which precedes shot #14, is used to suggest the passage of time. Dissolves two and three (before and after shot #22), however, serve to introduce and conclude the escape fantasy that the fugitive has while he is waiting in the park. Notice also the transitions that are used to link the fantasy to reality. The travel ad in the newspaper suggests the idea of the fantasy and the lighting of the cigarette concludes it.

Not only does this scene alter time, it also manipulates space. This is particularly true toward the conclusion, when the script calls for a series of shots (#35 through #38) that are widely separated spatially.

The editing style is based on continuity principles in those portions of the script (roughly the first half) that employ a relatively static point of view and emphasize continuity. The latter half of the scene, however, demands dynamic editing; the emphasis becomes dramatic, and in shots #25 through #43 a montage sequence is employed.

This script makes very little use of special visual effects. In shot #38, a "super" is employed to suggest the simultaneous coordinated activities of the police throughout the city. It is possible that a similar effect could be obtained by use of the split-screen montage; it would have the effect of heightening the number of activities that the police were involved in, but at the same time it would introduce an "unnatural" visual technique into a film which is predominantly a "realistic" depiction of action.

Finally, it should be noticed that nearly every shot in the script contains an element of continuity that links it to the following shot. In shot #25, for example, the man's eyes turn to the right and, in the following shot, the fugitive sees what the man is looking at—the detective who is partially hidden behind the bush. Likewise, in shot #35, the policeman who is stationed on the roof of the building raises the two-way radio to his lips and, in the succeeding shot, the audience sees the person he is speaking to—the police switchboard operator.

The success or failure of this scene is greatly dependent on the events that precede it. If the audience is aware that the fugitive has been set up by the informer, then nearly every activity of the scene will contain elements of latent danger. On the other hand, if the audience is not forewarned of the trap, the element of surprise will be present, but the early parts of the scene might seem static and boring.

Contemporary cinema appears to be moving toward a richer, denser depiction of experience. Having at last freed itself from the conventions of the theater, film has begun to take advantage of the uniqueness of its medium. Conventional editorial techniques of transitions and continuity are slowly being abandoned in favor of a more elliptical style. The pace of films, as well, has accelerated considerably; some of the cuts in *The Pawnbroker* and *Easy Rider,* for instance, verge on the subliminal but, amazingly, the viewer is able to grasp and understand what he has seen. Split-screen montage, used by film makers at least as far back as 1915 when Griffith made *The Birth of a Nation,* has reappeared as a viable visual technique (for example, Norman Jewison's *The Thomas Crown Affair* [1968] and Michael Wadleigh's *Woodstock* [1970]). In addition, some of the techniques of the experimentalists are finding their way into the narrative film: electronically produced sound (*Patton*) and highly sophisticated uses of cinematic technology (the Stargate Corridor sequence in *2001: A Space Odyssey*). In essence, the ever-increasing technical sophistication of the contemporary film suggests that today's film makers have the means to introduce subtleties or relate narratives that, yesterday, would simply have been impossible.

REFERENCES

1. V. I. Pudovkin, *Film Technique and Film Acting* (Hackensack, N.J.: Vision Press, 1958), p. 73.

2. Truffaut, François, *Hitchcock* (New York: Simon and Schuster, 1966), pp. 197–98.

3. Pudovkin, p. 23.

4. Ibid., p. 84.

5. Andrew Sarris, ed., *Interviews with Film Directors* (New York: Bobbs-Merrill, 1957), p. 398.

6. For an excellent overview of both the history of editing and a fine introduction to the editorial art, see Karel Reisz' *The Technique of Film Editing* (New York: Focal Press, 1958).

7. For a more detailed description of Porter's *The Life of an American Fireman* see Lewis Jacobs' *The Rise of the American Film* (New York: Harcourt Brace Jovanovich, 1939).

8. Most of Eisenstein's observations on film theory can be found in his two volumes *Film Sense* and *Film Form* (New York: Meridian Books, 1942 and 1949).

9. Pudovkin, p. 117.

10. Ibid., p. 169.

When audiences actually heard Al Jolson singing *Mammy*, they were also hearing the death knell for the so-called silent era of films. Here is a shot from the first "talkie," Warner Brothers' 1927 *The Jazz Singer*.

Courtesy of The Museum of Modern Art/Film Stills Archive

In order to evoke a sense of the 50s, Peter Bogdanovich made extensive use of the popular music of that decade in his *The Last Picture Show* (1971).

Courtesy of Columbia Pictures

4

APPEAL
TO THE EAR:

SOUND

▚ Life is inseparable from sound. ▛
SIEGFRIED KRACAUER[1]

D ESPITE the fact that the addition of sound was the single most important technical innovation in the first thirty years of film's history, it caused the film, as an art form, to revert to a stage of crudity that was paralleled only by the first of the silent films. When Warner Brothers released their first "talkie," *The Jazz Singer* with Al Jolson, in the latter part of 1927, the death knell for the so-called silent era had been tolled.[2]

The enthusiasm for pictures that talked was almost as great as the earlier enthusiasm for pictures that moved. By 1929, a little over a year after the release of *The Jazz Singer,* nearly every major motion picture in the United States talked. The motivation prompting the rapid conversion to sound was fairly obvious: paid admissions to the theaters, by 1929, had nearly doubled. The "talkies" were clearly ascendent, the "silents" eclipsed.

The term "silent" as a descriptive label for thirty years of movie making is somewhat misleading, however, for it suggests that early audiences viewed films that were totally devoid of sound. But completely silent films were the exception rather than the rule. Nearly every important motion picture, as well as a large percentage of less significant films, utilized some sort of musical score. For example, D. W. Griffith's *Birth of a Nation,* which was first shown to audiences in February 1915, was accompanied by an original symphonic score by Joseph Carl Breil, performed by an orchestra of seventy musical instruments. Even in "smaller" theaters, it was common practice for a trio of musicians to provide musical background for early films. However, prior to the entry of the "talkies," many theaters began to replace the musicians with an organist who accompanied the film on the recently developed Wurlitzer—varying the mood of his selections in accordance with the action of the different scenes. Even today, an occasional Wurlitzer can still be seen in some of the older and larger theaters.

The use of music during the silent era was prompted by both practical and aesthetic considerations. Any gathering of people, even in a theater, is to some extent a noisy affair: patrons shift in their seats, scrape their chairs, cough and talk. Aside from the clamor of the audience, there was the machinery of the early projectors to contend with; they produced an audible and distracting whirring sound. Musical accompaniment, in part, resolved these intrusive sounds by providing a backdrop of sound that not only muted undesirable noises but also had the effect of welding a collection of individuals into a unified audience.

But the music did not serve merely as a blanket of sound. Siegfried Kracauer, in his *Theory of Film,* points out that the music remained even though the noisy projectors were removed from the theater and placed in soundproof projection rooms.[3]

For some time silent film makers had been attracted to music because they recognized its dramatic potential. Music, it was clear, could create an atmosphere, suggest an emotion (joy, fear, grief, triumph), or heighten meaning by counterpointing a visual image with a contrasting musical score. For example, the screen might reveal an important, dignified character carrying out some serious task; yet a syncopated musical accompaniment could suggest that the character's actions were pompous and comic. Music, as might be expected, was relatively unaffected by the coming of sound. It weathered the transition from silent to sound films to become an even more integral aspect of the film experience.

Although the advent of sound, in retrospect, was abrupt and unheralded, it had been in the offing for a long time. Even before the turn of the twentieth century, there had already been several successful short talking films produced in Europe. In America, Thomas Edison's continued experimentation with the sound film was spurred primarily by his desire to find a device that would produce images to accompany his "talking" machine, the Victrola.

Sound was much more than a novel innovation, however. It was the key development that enabled film makers to correct many of the obvious artistic shortcomings inherent in the films of the silent era.

The most obvious advantage of sound was that it meant the elimination of subtitles and captions. There were, of course, a number of silent films that made little use of subtitles or captions (F. W. Murnau's *The Last Laugh* [1924], for instance, used none at all), but they were the exceptions rather than the rule. To most directors, the subtitles constituted a necessary evil, though they clearly presented him with problems. First, they represented a jarring interruption in the succession of visual images, making it nearly impossible for the director to establish and maintain a subtle rhythmic flow, and slowing the development of the action. Second, there was usually a marked incongruity between the images and the transcription of the action in the subtitle. For example, an audience might watch a couple ranting and raving at each other for several minutes, then read this masterpiece of understatement summarizing the scene: "They part in anger." Third, as an incidental side effect, audiences would be distracted by people who had missed the subtitle whispering to their friends, "What did it say?"

As Ralph Stephenson and J. R. Debrix suggest in *Cinema as Art*, "The introduction of sound freed the image to be itself, in other words, relieved it of the need to try and express sounds in visual terms."[4] From the inception of the silent film, film makers had had to struggle with the problem of finding visual equivalents for sounds. Cutting from a shot of a gossipy ladies' luncheon to a shot of a gaggle of geese adequately conveys the atmosphere of the luncheon by means of a film metaphor, but, at the same time, the unique quality of the luncheon is lost. With sound, the film maker was much better equipped to create a stronger sense of factual reality.

The sound film also made it possible for the director to extend the boundaries of the screen beyond what was actually depicted. In the days of the silent film, if a film maker wished to portray the gossipy ladies' luncheon, he would have had to film most of the action by means of medium-long shots; visually this would convey the desired effect of many women speaking at once. With sound, however, he could pick out, in close-up, two ladies who best characterized the stereotyped gossips; their conversation could dominate the foreground of sound, while microphones recorded other conversations for background sound. Though the viewer was only *watching* two women, he would be simultaneously aware, through the sound track, of the presence of all the other women.

In addition to enlarging the scene of action, sound also enabled the film maker to increase the density of the film experience. There is something incongruous about watching a character standing on a busy corner in New York City in a silent film. The accompaniment of sound—the noises of the city streets—would not only enrich the reality of this scene but would also convey a strong sense of place, enabling the film maker to build up the detail of a given scene without having to show the viewer the source of every sound.

The addition of sound caused the film to become far more complex, both technically and artistically. That sound would create an abundance of technical problems almost goes without saying, but the development of sound was simultaneously accompanied by more subtle and complex delineation of character. During the silent era, a psychological study was a rarity. The "silents," because of their technical limitations, were forced to deal with character depiction on a relatively superficial basis. Revelation of character had to be achieved almost entirely in visual terms; the villain was easily recognized as the guy who always kicked the defenseless dog, twisted his waxed moustache, or foreclosed on the widow. The hero, on the other hand, patted dogs on the head, helped old ladies across the street, and always shaved. Even though a look, a gesture, or a movement can provide subtle commentary on characterization, visual revelation of character is necessarily limited. Sound offered the film maker the means by which he could avoid clichés, and explore character in depth.

And yet despite the numerous possibilities that the addition of sound had opened up, the early sound films were pedestrian and disappointing. Film appeared to have regressed to the primitiveness of the first of the silent films. The reasons for this were both technical and economic.

Converting to sound was an expensive proposition, further complicated by the fact that the sound film was developed just prior to and during the Depression. Understandably, there was some hesitancy on the part of the studios and theater owners to convert their facilities for sound. Everyone wanted to be sure that the sound system would not only work properly, but would also prove to be popular with the public. As it turned out, those studios that resisted the transition met with economic disaster, for audiences soon demanded talking films. Although the finances were made available for the transition to sound by various moneyed interests, there was usually a string attached. The investors insisted on having one of their representatives sit on the board of the motion picture studio. Thus, men who had no experience whatsoever in film were placed in policy-making positions.

Within a year after the advent of sound, the entire makeup of the film industry had undergone radical changes. Convinced that it was the spoken word that was attracting the larger audiences, Hollywood began a large-scale recruiting program to bring in stage directors from Broadway, as well as playwrights and actors with theatrical backgrounds. Suddenly, many of the directors of the silent era found themselves out of work. Similarly, a number of popular silent screen actors and actresses became unemployable because of foreign accents, peculiar voice qualities, or awkward diction. At least temporarily, the distinctive cinematic qualities of film appeared lost; the early sound films amounted to little more than "canned theater."

But the most crippling blow to the industry was dealt by the tyrannical sound expert and his omnipresent microphone. As noted earlier, one of the significant breakthroughs in the development of film was the freeing of the camera from its fixed position. Sound changed all that, making the camera once again static and immobile. The early cameras were noisy pieces of machinery; their gears set up a din that was readily picked up by the microphones. To inhibit the noise, they were placed in a soundproof box, referred to as the "ice box," and once again, the action was staged as it would be in a theater.

The microphone itself was another shackle. It was the sound expert, rather than the director, who decided where the actors would be placed and which shots could be taken; artistic considerations were suddenly made subservient to the demands of sound. The result was a tiresome parade of incredibly static, stagy, talky motion pictures that were replete with every conceivable sound known to man. The artistry and subtlety realized in the best of the silent films appeared to be lost forever.

But, fortunately, the "canned theater" debacle didn't prevail for long. A group of talented and creative directors such as Ernst Lubitsch, Reuben Mamoulian, Lewis Milestone, and King Vidor began to discover the means by which they could circumvent the tyranny of sound.

The major discovery (attributed to Ernst Lubitsch by critic Arthur Knight[5]) was that a film did not have to involve talking *throughout,* nor did the sound have to be recorded synchronously; the audio could be added later or "dubbed in." The breakthrough was significant. The camera could now be freed from the imprisonment of the soundproof box; it could be taken "off ice." That sound could be added later also implied that the techniques developed during the silent era were still valid; the camera could once again move unimpaired from long shot to close-up, and silent-editing techniques were as viable as before. Dubbing also made it possible for the camera to extend its range. Previously, outdoor shots had been technical nightmares for sound technicians because there was an excess of intrusive sound (wind noises, leaves rustling, and so on) that frequently drowned out the lines of the actors. The actors as well enjoyed new freedom, for they were not entirely limited by the hearing range of the microphones.

Not only was the director able to resume his rightful role in the film process, but he also discovered that he could bring sound, like the visual image, under his control. Prior to the post-synchronous recording of sound, nearly every sound on the set was transcribed verbatim. The extreme density of noise and music had the effect of undermining the visuals of the film. But because the director was able to become more selective in his use of sound, the visuals could once again dominate the screen.

That the camera could be employed independently of sound suggested that sound could also be used independently of the image. The early trend in sound films was to record visually everything that made a noise—the viewer hears a ringing and simultaneously sees a bell. But in reality, many sounds emanate from unseen sources: a plane flying overhead, a train in the distance, or a dog baying at the moon. Using sounds whose sources lay outside the range of the camera not only extended the scope of the film experience but also made it possible for the director to establish a mood, suggest a place, or oppose an image with a contrary sound. Film makers began to examine the creative potential of sound. The adoption of the interior monologue was just one of the results of their study.

Soon after the introduction of sound came a rash of theoretical proclamations concerning its proper use in film. Some of the more articulate theorists were Russians Sergei Eisenstein, V. I. Pudovkin and G. Alexandrov, and Frenchman René Clair.

Understandably, Eisenstein, Pudovkin, and Alexandrov viewed sound as a means of extending their theories of montage. In 1930, Eisenstein drew up a manifesto, which was signed by Pudovkin and Alexandrov. It read, in part:

The success of Soviet films on the world's screen is due, to a significant degree, to those methods of montage which they first revealed and consolidated.

Therefore, for the further development of the cinema, the important moments will be only those that strengthen and broaden the montage methods of affecting the spectator.

ONLY A CONTRAPUNTAL USE of sound in relation to the visual montage piece will afford a new potentiality of montage development and perfection.

THE FIRST EXPERIMENTAL WORK WITH SOUND MUST BE DIRECTED ALONG THE LINE OF ITS DISTINCT NON-SYNCHRONIZATION WITH VISUAL IMAGES.[6]

Eisenstein felt that the real value of sound lay in its ability to create new cinematic forms; the director could orchestrate sound contrapuntally with the visual images, rather than slavishly synchronizing a sound to an image in a realistic manner. Pudovkin, on another occasion, pointed out that in life, sound rarely parallels the visual image we see. We don't, he observed, gaze at a speaker fixedly; rather, our eyes shift around, observing first one thing, then another; periodically, our eyes will return to the speaker.

Similarly, in France, René Clair was making his own contribution to the theory of sound. Like the Russians, Clair felt that sound need not restrict itself to a faithful transcription of reality. Clair observed that the early "talkies," which recorded nearly every available sound, produced an artificial effect.[7] Thus, he concluded, a sound should be selected as carefully as an image: which particular sound or sounds were used should be determined by the demands of the scene. The ear, he felt, was as discriminating toward a sound as the eye was to an image. In a battle scene, for instance, the protagonist's mind might well blot out the din of explosions and gunfire and be conscious only of the labored breathing of his wounded comrade. In his own films, Clair avoided sound that held only novelty interest and searched, instead, for sounds that helped the viewer better understand the action.

In the late twenties and early thirties, developments in sound engineering were making it technically possible for film makers to employ sound more creatively. The noiseless camera was soon perfected and existing recording equipment became more sophisticated. However, there still remained the problem of developing a more positive means of synchronizing sound and image.

In their initial forays into sound, Warner Brothers had relied on wax disks. Although the disks did provide the means to synchronize sound and image, they were far from satisfactory. Frequently, the sound would get out of "sync," causing the audio to lag behind or run ahead of the image. The first real breakthrough in synchronization came with the development of the optical sound track. With this method, the sound could now be scribed directly onto the film; this eliminated duplication of equipment, and ensured perfect synchronization.

In the optical sound process, the microphones record the sound, and the recorded sound is then translated into electrical impulses. These electrical impulses are "photographed" as visual patterns which are in turn scribed alongside the visual images. (The parallel white lines to the right of the images on pages 62 to 65 represent the optical sound track.) The projector "reads" these images by means of a scanning light, and the visual pattern is reconverted to the originally recorded sounds. The optical sound track remained in use throughout the 1940s. In the 1950s magnetic tape, which made immediate playback possible, superseded optical sound. Today, magnetic tape is still the most common method of recording and editing sound.

In today's cinema, the use of sound can be described in terms of four major areas: synchronous sound, asynchronous sound, silence, and music.

Synchronous sound (from the Greek word *sunkhronos: sun* meaning *same,* and *khronos* meaning *time*) is sound that corresponds directly to a pictured image. The viewer, in this instance, sees a character speaking and simultaneously hears what he is saying. Synchronous sound, as pointed out earlier, dominated the early sound films, where the emphasis was on the novelty of sound and virtually everything that made a noise was pictured. Although synchronous sound is probably the least imaginative use of sound, it is also obviously the most necessary and frequently employed type.

Asynchronous sound, on the other hand, relates to a source that is off-camera. To use Pudovkin's example again, the viewer *hears* the speaker but *sees* the person he is addressing. The uses of asynchronous sound are limitless. A character, in the course of conversation, might mention San Francisco and the viewer see on the screen an image of a cable car or the Golden Gate Bridge. Or the screen could show an image of a woman screaming, but the spectator hears the shrill wail of a siren. Or perhaps there is a shot of two small children fighting, but the sound track carries the cacophony of war.

There is an extremely interesting use of sound in Alain Resnais' *Hiroshima, Mon Amour* (1959). Below, in an excerpt from Part One of Marguerite Duras' scenario for the film, an unnamed Frenchwoman and a Japanese engineer or architect "discuss" Hiroshima.

He: You saw nothing in Hiroshima. Nothing.

(To be used as often as desired. A woman's voice, also
flat, muffled, monotonous, the voice of someone
reciting, replies:)

She: I saw everything. Everything.

(Fusco's music, which has faded before this initial
exchange, resumes just long enough to accompany the woman's
hand tightening on the shoulder again, then letting go,
then caressing it. The mark of fingernails on the darker
flesh. As if this scratch could give the illusion of being
a punishment for: "No. You saw nothing in Hiroshima." Then
the woman's voice begins again, still calm, colorless,
incantatory:)

She: The hospital, for instance, I saw it. I'm sure I did.
     There is a hospital in Hiroshima. How could I help
     seeing it?

(The hospital, hallways, stairs, patients, the camera
coldly objective. (We never see her seeing.) Then we come
back to the hand gripping--and not letting go of--the
darker shoulder.)

He: You did not see the hospital at Hiroshima. You saw
    nothing at Hiroshima.

(Then the woman's voice becomes--more impersonal. Shots of
the museum. The same blinding light, the same ugly light
here as at the hospital. Explanatory signs, pieces of
evidence from the bombardment, scale models, mutilated
iron, skin, burned hair, wax models, etc.)

She: Four times at the museum . . .

He: What museum in Hiroshima?

She: Four times at the museum in Hiroshima. I saw people
    walking around. The people walk around, lost in
    thought, among the photographs, the reconstructions,
    for want of something else, among the photographs, the
    photographs, the reconstructions, for want of
    something else, the explanations, for want of
    something else. . . .[8]

The conception and realization of this scene are brilliant.
Dramatically portraying one of the most ghastly atrocities in the
history of mankind without succumbing to either sentimentality
or propaganda is no mean feat. Duras' scenario succeeds by
means of a subtle use of asynchronous sound supported by carefully selected images.

The camera reveals that the man and the woman, both naked,
are in bed. Nudity not only dramatizes the frailty and defense-
lessness of the couple, but also recalls the helplessness of the
victims of Hiroshima. The flat, colorless voices preclude sentimentality and yet convincingly portray the devastating effect
that the bombing of Hiroshima has had on the speakers' sensibilities. The incantatory repetition, readily apparent in the
woman's last speech, underwrites the feeling of despair. The use
of synchronous sound, in this instance, makes a significant contribution to our understanding of the visual images. The shots
of the hospital and the museum are, of course, asynchronous to
the dialogue. Although the man denies that the woman has seen
anything, the reality of the shots of the hospital and museum
are indelibly etched into the memory of the spectator. The
woman's affirmation of what she has seen, followed by the man's
denial, may appear perplexing, but the exchange succinctly
conveys the impossibility of "talking about" Hiroshima.

The advantages of asynchronous sound are fairly apparent. It can either provide additional support for an image, as in a shot of a bombed-out village accompanied by a forlorn scream; or counterpart an image—for instance, by showing an image of an empty football stadium and recording the cheering of the crowds. A dramatic instance of this latter use occurs in John S. Avidsen's *Save the Tiger* (1973). The protagonist (played by Jack Lemmon) stands on an empty California beach recalling the fighting at Anzio Beach in southern Italy in 1944. The audience begins to hear a crescendo of battle sounds—cries and explosions, muted at first, then intensifying to a roar. The impact could not be more vivid if the film maker had actually depicted the soldiers and tanks on the screen behind Lemmon.

Asynchronous sound has also been employed in some films as a transitional device. In Larry Peerce's *Goodbye, Columbus* (1969), for example, the film's protagonist, Neil, is seen in conversation with his aunt. As this scene fades out and another showing Neil driving across town fades in, their conversation continues on the sound track. In addition to bridging the two scenes, this particular use of sound seems to suggest that the conversation remains in Neil's mind even though he has physically left his aunt behind him.

Silence is usually thought of as a negative value—the absence of sound. Ironically, it was the sound film that made it possible for silence to attain positive value. Handled appropriately, silence can have significant dramatic impact on an audience. If silence precedes an action, it tends to highlight the moment, set it within a dramatic frame. In a courtroom, the man on trial stands to defend himself, and the courtroom becomes hushed and attentive as it awaits his speech. A woman is sitting in a near-empty room, waiting for a man who she has reason to believe might kill her. The silence of her vigil will be heavily laden with tension for the audience. Silence can also be employed to impart a quality of strangeness, even of horror, to the familiar. A busy street corner, deprived of familiar noises, becomes, somehow, a threatening, alien landscape. As might be assumed from the previous examples, the use of silence in a film is frequently associated with tension, suspense, and danger. Michelangelo Antonioni, for example, made use of huge "blocks" of silence in his highly acclaimed *Blowup* (1967).

The advent of the sound film created a more aurally sensitive audience as well. The quality of a sound became nearly as important as the rendering of an image. One significant change for the better was in the film use of dialogue. Silent films tended to employ a dialogue that was pompous, artificial, and theatrical in nature. The subtitles represented an intrusive interruption of the film experience; consequently, the tendency was to keep subtitles to a minimum, including only enough information to make the visuals understandable to the audience. When sound arrived, dialogue was no longer intrusive, but integral; and it made very different demands on the writer than the dialogue of the "silents," or even of stage plays.

Language, in the theater, represents a significant aspect of the dramatic experience. The plays of Shakespeare, Marlowe, Sheridan, Yeats, Eliot, and others of similar stature are studied as great works of literature. The reason is fairly obvious: the language of drama is highly expressive. But because of the inherent differences in the theatrical and film experiences, the sound film requires a substantially different language. Theater tends to employ more artifice than film; its audience accepts certain conventions—the removal of the fourth wall, stage whispers, soliloquies, scenery—as part of the theatrical experience. Thus, rhetorical language often seems appropriate to theater art. But the conventions of cinema are not the same. Film tends to be more "realistic" than theater. Furthermore—because of the camera's ability to move within inches of a subject and portray the action from the vantage point of the protagonist, and even, in some instances, to delineate subjective states of consciousness —the film, in this sense, represents a more intimate genre. Consequently, the dialogue of film has to be lifelike: its language must closely approximate everyday speech. The film maker's art is also primarily a visual art, and when meaning can be conveyed by images, action, or gestures, dialogue becomes superfluous. Even the most cursory comparison of the script of a play and a scenario for a film will reveal that the speeches in stage plays tend to be two to three times as long as equivalent speeches in film. (It will also be observed that the meaning of the play is discoverable within its language alone—clearly, this is not the case with film.) Thus, the representative dialogue of today's films tends to be terse, understated, and above all, realistic.

A classic case of the disparity between literary dialogue and screen dialogue occurred in a much-publicized encounter between novelist F. Scott Fitzgerald and director Joseph L. Mankiewicz in the late '30s. Fitzgerald had written the dialogue for a film entitled *Three Comrades;* one of the film's actresses, Margaret Sullavan, complained that most of the lines were literally unspeakable, so Mankiewicz himself rewrote much of the dialogue. Fitzgerald was enraged and promptly wrote Mankiewicz.

> For nineteen years with two years out for sickness, I've written best-selling entertainment, and my dialogue is supposedly right up at the top. But I've learned from the script that you've suddenly decided that it isn't good dialogue and you can take a few hours off and do much better.[9]

Mankiewicz argued, however, that the changes he made "cast [no] more of a reflection on Fitzgerald's novels than the bad plays of Henry James cast on his great novels."[10] Mankiewicz attempted to define the difference between writing a novel and writing for the screen:

> The novelist has an entirely different relationship with his reader than the screenwriter [or playwright] has with his audience. With a book, the relationship is between the printed page and the reader's intellect. The response is cerebral. On the screen [and the stage], the dialogue is heard, there is no time for cerebration— the response is to the rhythm and sound of the speech almost as much as to its content.[11]

The film maker, in addition to learning to cope with the written word, had to contend with other factors. He had to make sure, for example, that the dialogue matched the image. In the theater, nearly all dialogue originates from approximately the same position, the confines of the stage. But in the film, actors are frequently widely separated spatially. The film maker needs to be sure that the voice of a character who is standing twenty-five feet from the camera *sounds* as though he were twenty-five feet away. The sound must be proportionate to the image. And unlike the dramatist, who deals almost entirely with dialogue, the film maker must orchestrate incidental noise as well as music.

As was mentioned earlier, music has always represented a significant aspect of the film experience. When sound was intro-

duced, the changes in the use of music were not so much quantitative as qualitative. The optical sound track, which ensured
perfect synchronization of sound and image, raised the use of
music in film to the status of a subtle art. Even in the days of
the "silent" film, music had been successfully employed to suggest
a mood or augment the drama of a particular scene, but now
music could expand the reality of a shot as well as sustain dramatically important musical motifs. For example, if the camera
pans the streets of Bombay as the audience listens to sitar music,
the "atmosphere," or the feeling of being in Bombay, is intensi-
fied. Again, if a young man is beaten nearly senseless by a group
of hoodlums behind a dance hall, the recurrence of the song that
the band was playing at the time of the beating has the effect
of recalling the incident for the audience as well as for the
young man.

Although music represents a more "unnatural" use of sound
than dialogue or noise, it is susceptible to the principles of synchronous and asynchronous sound. Obviously, if the audience
sees a trio of musicians playing and simultaneously hears jazz,
the use of music is synchronous. Likewise, it might be argued
that a shot of a riverboat making its way down the Mississippi
accompanied by strains of "Old Man River" would also be synchronous; for the use of sound, in this instance, is predictably
supportive and offers no additional information. However, if the
screen represents two jet fighters engaged in a dogfight and the
accompanying sound track plays a stately minuet, the effect is
quite different. The visuals represent one thing (two planes engaged in aerial combat), the sound track another (seventeenth-
century dance music); but the combination becomes a metaphor
describing the action of the planes as a sardonically grim dance
of death.

The above example represents a more imaginative use of
sound than merely recording the scream of jet engines and the
rattle of machine-gun fire. Used creatively, sound is generally
either independent of or supportive to the image, rather than
duplicative of it.

It is also possible, for example, for a film maker to replace
a shot with a sound. If there is a critical scene in which the
protagonist of the film, a woman, is being deserted by the man
she loves, it is far more dramatically effective to hold the camera
on her distressed face as the man walks out, slamming the door

behind him, than to actually show the man's departure. The sound of the slammed door makes it unnecessary to show him leaving and, more importantly, the audience wants to see the woman's response.

Frequently, a film maker will alter sound for dramatic emphasis. In a film about competitive amateur snow skiing called *Downhill Racer* (1970), there are several shots which show how a dangerous downhill run appears from the vantage point of the skier. The sole portion of the racer that is visible in the frame are the tips of his skis; the audience hears only his labored breathing. Obviously, in reality, other sounds would be present, but their omission and the stress on the racer's breathing emphasize the arduousness of the run. Likewise, if the protagonist of a film is lost in the woods at night, exaggerating the cries of animals, the crackling of twigs, and the sound of the wind in the trees is not only dramatically effective but psychologically legitimate, for it approximates the way the character would intensify these vaguely threatening noises in his mind.

Synthetic sound, which represents electronically produced noises that have no counterpart in reality, is another important source of creative sound. Here, sound is attained in unorthodox ways: by running tapes backward, by mixing and overlaying sounds from disparate sources, by recording the noises of various pieces of electronic equipment and orchestrating them into musical motifs. Thus far, the use of synthetic sound has been restricted to relatively limited areas: science fiction and the aural depiction of altered or abnormal states of consciousness and fantasy. But it is obvious that the presence of electronic sound in our everyday lives is steadily increasing. It can be predicted with some surety that synthetic sound and electronic music will widen their sphere of influence in the coming years.

Inasmuch as sound, on film, is represented by optical patterns, some film makers have experimented by directly scribing the sound onto the film without benefit of recording equipment. One of the pioneers in this area is Canadian film maker Norman McLaren. McLaren, who employs this technique in two of his award-winning short subjects, *Dots* and *Loops*, created a whole new range of sound possibilities with this method. Although his technique obviously has great potential, it would appear that its limited applications, compounded by the considerable investment of time required to hand-scribe the sound track, would necessarily prohibit widespread usage.

Though it is difficult to draw up any dogmatic rules governing the function of sound in film, it is possible to indicate what comprises ineffective usage. Symbolic use of sound, for instance, should be comprehensible to a reasonably perceptive member of the audience. For example, if a film maker portrays a couple having a marvelous time riding a cable car in San Francisco, but attempts to foreshadow the forthcoming end of this gaiety by means of a mournful wail of a siren faintly heard in the background, the chances are that the effect will be completely lost on the audience. The viewer, responding to the couple's gaiety, will perceive the noise of the siren as just one more of many similar sounds that convey the total atmosphere of the city. On the other hand, the film maker might show the same couple seated in an outdoor restaurant quietly talking, and have the woman say, "I can't remember being happier. I keep telling myself that it can't last," and there follows a quiet moment as the two look at each other. In the interim of silence, the wail of the siren is discernible in the background. Preceded by the woman's comment about happiness, the distant siren strikes an ominous note, and the symbolic message is clear: happiness is a transitory state, at best.

The creative potential of asynchronous sound in films is virtually unlimited; the film maker, however, must be very careful not to confuse his audience when he employs unusual juxtapositions of sound with images. For instance, if the film maker shows the audience shots of commuters being herded into subway trains by conductors and simultaneously plays the sounds of lowing cattle, the juxtaposition of sound and image is comprehensible. On the other hand, the audience may witness a scene in which a young man is being taunted and ridiculed by his elders; he stalks from the room slamming the door behind him. Rather than hearing the slam of a door, the audience hears the sharp report of a pistol shot; later in the film, the audience learns that the young man has gravitated to a life of crime. The sound of the pistol shot is an attempt to relate the young man's humiliation to his eventual choice of occupation, but the audience's response to that sound will probably be one of perplexity. The suggested relationship between the scene and the shot, tenuous at best, requires either further elaboration or total elimination.

Even from this brief discussion of sound, it should be clear that creative and effective use of sound in film does not necessarily mean exact duplication of the sounds we hear in everyday life. Sound, in film, is characterized by selectivity and restraint; in real life, by contrast, we are subject to a constant bombardment of random and usually meaningless noises—the whine of tires against pavement, the labored drone of a truck engine, the periodic shriek of a siren, the whisper of a jet passing overhead, voices, radios, television, birds, machines, wind, rain, and so on. But the film maker's decision to ignore these extraneous noises is not an arbitrary one. In any given situation that involves a choice, we, too, choose to differentiate between the superfluous and the significant. As gestalt psychologists would say, we select from the total configuration of experience a figure that commands our attention. Everything else recedes to the status of the less important background. Effective use of sound, then, represents a departure from or variation on reality.

The skillful application of sound can also be evaluated in terms of what it contributes to the effectiveness of the image. Does the sound merely duplicate the image, explaining to the audience aurally what has already been understood visually, or does the sound increase perception of meaning? Can it, for example, intensify the image's significance? Imagine a camera panning a section of a polluted stream, objectively recording man's senseless contamination of his environment; the audience hears only the anguished wail of a small child—the recipient of this dubious heritage. Or perhaps the audience witnesses a small crowd encouraging two young boys to fight. The sounds of shouting from the crowd give way to the sounds of war. In this instance, the meaning of the image has been extended by the sound track. The juxtaposition of sound and image seems to suggest that society, represented by the crowd surrounding the two boys, encourages violence and that war represents the logical culmination of this behavior.

The sound film, now forty years old, is still undergoing change. Electronic sound and music as well as hand-scribed sound tracks are subjects of constant experimentation by underground and university film makers. Stereophonic sound, now used in all Cinerama productions as well as many conventional films, augments an audience's experience of "being there" through the use of multiple sound tracks and speakers. Michael

Wadleigh's documentary/celebration, *Woodstock* (1970), for example, represents an outstanding example of how the contemporary film maker can use multiple sound tracks to create the illusion of sound in depth. The sophisticated recording and playback equipment of the larger studios make it very probable that future audiences will experience total sound environments as part of the film experience. Multiple-track recording channeled through speakers placed throughout an auditorium could reproduce the complex sound spectrum of a modern city or the subtle interplay of sounds that occur when a sailboat tacks across a bay. Although a total sound environment could represent an exciting film experience for an audience, it could also retrogress to mere novelty interest. Any technical innovation should ultimately be subservient to an artist's creativity and vision. When technique becomes an end in itself, the art of the film suffers.

REFERENCES

1. Siegfried Kracauer, *Theory of Film* (New York: Oxford University Press, 1960), p. 134.

2. For a more detailed account of the emergence and subsequent development of the sound film, see Arthur Knight's *The Liveliest Art* (New York: New American Library, 1957).

3. Kracauer, p. 133.

4. Ralph Stephenson and J. R. Debrix, *The Cinema as Art* (Baltimore: Penguin Books, 1965), p. 183.

5. Arthur Knight, *The Liveliest Art* (New York: New American Library, 1957), p. 151.

6. Sergei Eisenstein, *Film Form* and *The Film Sense* (Cleveland: Meridian, 1957), *Film Form*, pp. 257–58.

7. Richard Dyer MacCann, ed., *Film: A Montage of Theories* (New York: Dutton, 1966), p. 39.

8. Marguerite Duras and Alain Resnais, *Hiroshima, Mon Amour* (New York: Evergreen, 1961), pp. 15–17.

9. Andrew Sarris, "Mankiewicz of The Movies," *Show* (March, 1970), p. 29.

10. Ibid., p. 29.

11. Ibid.

Recently, films such as Sydney Pollack's *They Shoot Horses, Don't They?* (1970) and Bernardo Bertolucci's *The Last Tango in Paris* (1973) have made use of the dance as a metaphor for life. This still, taken from *They Shoot Horses, Don't They?* portrays life as a ruthless and competitive marathon dance.

5

FIGURATIVE LANGUAGE:

FILM AND LITERATURE

> Nothing can resist the unifying power of the metaphor; anything conceivable by the human mind can be compared to something else.
>
> PIER PAOLO PASOLINI[1]

John Cassavetes' *Faces* (1968), discussed in chapter 2, brutally depicts the frustration and not-so-quiet despair of a middle-class American couple at mid-century.

Courtesy of Walter Reade 16, 241 East 34th Street, New York City, N.Y. 10016

"All Animals Are Equal but Some Animals Are More Equal Than Others," says Comrade Pig in the 1955 feature-length cartoon of George Orwell's allegory, *Animal Farm.*

Courtesy of Contemporary Films/McGraw-Hill

Quite often in a film a landscape becomes freighted with symbolic meaning. Here is a shot from Michelangelo Antonioni's 1960 *L'Avventura* (see pp. 125–126).

Courtesy of Janus Films, Inc.

In comparison to the jaded, decadent characters who populate Fellini's *La Dolce Vita* (1959), the young girl in the café near the seashore stands out as a symbol of purity and innocence.

Courtesy of Macmillan Audio Brandon

I N THE PRECEDING chapters, the considerations of meaning in film were, for the most part, allied with the artist's use of technique. A film maker, for example, consciously selects a particular lens for a shot because he knows beforehand that its properties will cause an image to be presented in a particular way: a fisheye lens will make an image appear distorted and unrealistic, a telephoto lens used on a crowd will emphasize the crowd's density, and so on. If the film's theme demanded, the latter technique could be used to stress the crowded conditions of contemporary living in an overpopulated world. But the question of meaning, of course, is not reducible to technique alone. Rather, it is intimately related to the artist's vision, his way of seeing the world, his sense of moral or aesthetic values, his capacity to respond emotionally to situations, and his sensitivity to the nuances of language, whether it be the language of literature or the language of film.

A sensitive writer is conscious of the fact that most words have the potential for a double meaning: the denotative, or dictionary meaning, and the connotative meaning, which refers to any emotional associations the word may carry. For example, if a writer is attempting to describe a woman who is lean or slender of figure, any one of the following words would accomplish that task: "thin," "petite," or "scrawny." Each of the three words has approximately the same denotative meaning; however, the connotations of these words differ considerably. "Thin," for example, is a relatively neutral word that simply describes the individual's build. "Petite," on the other hand, moves in the direction of an implied judgment: it carries the positive connotations of delicate and fragile beauty. "Scrawny," however, implies a negative judgment—the image of a gaunt, bony, somewhat disheveled figure comes to mind. Which of these three possibilities the writer will ultimately select depends on how he wants the reader to perceive this particular character—neutrally, positively, or negatively.

Everyone, in the course of a day, will—at one point or another, consciously or unconsciously—weigh the connotations of a word before uttering it. Thus, it is relatively common practice to distinguish between a word's denotation and its connotation. Rarely, however, is an image considered in these terms; yet it is clear that an image, like a word, may well function on two levels.

In the previous example, the denotative value of the three words was approximately the same, but their connotations were quite different. Let us consider an image whose denotation will remain unaffected even though its connotations are altered. Imagine a wooden, two-storied Victorian house that was built just after the turn of the century on a steep hill in San Francisco. The building's straight, somewhat severe lines are broken up by beautiful and ornate woodwork that adorns the corners and eaves of the house. The house itself is painted avocado green and the trim is done in black. A huge, hand-carved wooden door with a leaded glass window dominates the front of the house. It looks as though it has about a dozen rooms. This brief, somewhat sketchy description would represent the quantitative, or denotative, meaning of an image of that house.

Assume that a film maker wishes to film three different takes of this same house, but he wants to alter the connotations in each take. For the first take, he might set up his camera across the street from the house. In the flat, colorless light of the noonday sun, he films the house as a passerby might see it. The resulting image is relatively neutral: the house appears to be a well-preserved architectural remnant of the past. The following day, at sunrise, the film maker records his second take of the house. This time he angles the camera in such a way as to emphasize the rich ornamental woodwork, and the jewel-like quality of the leaded glass window. The gold of the red-orange sun spills over the roof and sides of the house, framing it in a rich play of color. In this instance, the house acquires an air of nostalgia: the image calls up associations of a less harried, more genteel life-style, an existence that was, in many ways, less complicated and demanding than that of today's world. Later that same day, in the early hours of the evening, the film maker records his third and final take. This time, he moves the camera very close to the house and positions it so that it points upward at an unusual angle. In this take, the house appears very different. This unorthodox and low camera angle causes the viewer to look up at the house, which now seems overpowering and somehow intimidating. Since it is early in the evening, large areas of the house are in shadow; this also contributes to the feeling of mystery and eeriness. The house appears like a huge Gothic mansion, perhaps the scene of clandestine, mysterious, or evil rites.

In each of the three takes, the denotative, or literal, meaning of the image—a two-storied Victorian house—remains unchanged, but the connotations of the image are altered. The first portrays the house neutrally; the second romanticizes it; the third makes it seem mysterious and forbidding. The first take would easily lend itself to a documentary on San Francisco; the second, perhaps a shot from a musical or a comedy; the third, a story of horror or intrigue. By manipulating the *connotations* of the image, the film maker is not only able to convey more information within a given image, but he is also able to alter the emotional overtones of the image itself. Thus, as Italian film maker Pier Paolo Pasolini has noted, "an image can have an allusive force equivalent to that of a word, since it represents the culmination of a series of analogies, which is to say it is part of the total stylistic structure."[2]

In literature, connotation forms the basis of figurative language and literary tropes. Figurative language, which includes the metaphor, the simile, personification, paradox, hyperbole, and understatement, is a tremendously important aspect of the literary experience, for it provides the writer with the means to communicate far more than he ever could if he adhered exclusively to a literal use of language. Figurative language, a departure from the conventional and ordinary uses of words, enables the writer to coin a fresh or unique expression or perhaps even startle his reader into considering a subject in a new or unusual light.

Figures of speech, or literary tropes, are nonliteral uses of language. Robert Frost once said that "Poetry provides the one permissible way of saying one thing and meaning another." Frost's statement points up an important aspect of figurative language, namely, that it is able to illuminate one image by describing it in terms of something else. For example, if a person says, "It gets foggy at twilight," then he uses language in a conventional and informative sense. However, when Robert Frost writes "the fog comes in on little cat feet," he is using language in a figurative sense. The image of fog as a cat brings to mind those qualities that fog and cats have in common—mystery, softness, stealthiness. By using language figuratively, Frost communicates more about fog than the conventional description; in addition, his image is an extremely vivid and memorable one.

Connotation, it has been argued, is the basis of figurative language. If an image can be affected by connotation, and it appears as though it can, then it would be useful to consider whether there is such a thing as a figurative use of an image; and if so, whether there are equivalents in film for the metaphor, the simile, and related literary tropes.

In its broadest sense, a figurative image may be said to occur whenever a film maker, for the sake of emphasis or freshness, departs from the conventional way of filming a subject. Russian film maker and theoretician V. I. Pudovkin, for example, has argued that "to show something as everyone sees it is to have accomplished nothing." If, for instance, the film maker's subject is a group of wealthy women who are all attired in expensive clothes and elaborately plumed hats, the conventional way of filming them would probably be via an eye-level shot. But instead of filming the women in this manner, the film maker positions his camera so that it is directly above the women, pointed down on their hats. Thus, the viewer observes only the feathered plumage and the tops of their hats: and the women are portrayed as rare and exotic bird-like creatures. And in Roman Polanski's "Two Men and a Wardrobe," there is one initially baffling figurative image which shows what appears to be a fish flying through the air. Seconds later, however, a hand reaches into the frame and grabs the fish. The following full shot reveals that the two men had stopped for lunch and were sitting on their wardrobe, which had been set on its side. The fish, in turn, had been placed on a mirror mounted on the side of the wardrobe, which, in that position, reflected the sky overhead. Both of these shots could be considered examples of the figurative use of a camera; in both instances, the images are unorthodox and striking, and both convey more meaning than conventional shots.

In literary works, a very common figure of speech is the metaphor. Basically, the metaphor is an implied comparison between two things which are essentially unlike: "My love is a red rose." In an ordinary comparison, there is usually no departure from the conventional denotations of words ("A car is faster than a horse"), but the metaphor represents a richer, denser kind of comparison which, on a superficial level, seems to be illogical. How, for example, could a woman be a rose? Obviously the speaker does not mean to imply that the woman is underweight (stem-like body) and has an oversized head (the bloom), but wants to suggest a beauty that is delicate, soft, perhaps sweetly scented. When Jaques, a character in Shakespeare's *As You Like It,* says: "All the world's a stage/And all the men and women merely players. . . ." (II. vii. 739–40) he is suggesting by means of a metaphor that life itself works very much like a stage play: like actors, people have entrances and exits (births and deaths). He goes on to extend the comparison, observing that in the course of their lifetimes, men are apt to play many different roles: infant, schoolboy, lover, soldier, justice, mature man, senile old man.

Jaques' metaphor is expansive; that is, it takes the entire world as the basis of its comparison. Poet William Blake operates on an equally suggestive but more restricted basis when he says, "To see a world in a grain of sand. . . ." At first Blake's comparison appears to be contradictory: a grain of sand is very minute, so how could it possibly be compared to a world? But upon reflection, it appears that the analogy is a very logical one. In the immensity of the universe, the earth is of little more size or importance than a grain of sand; a grain of sand is shaped like a miniature model of the world; a grain of sand is common and ordinary and yet unique because there is no other grain exactly like it, as the earth is unique among all the planets of the universe.

In literature, the metaphor forces the reader to consider the similarities between two apparently dissimilar things. Frequently, the metaphor has the effect of helping the reader to make fresh or unusual discoveries for himself. Film, of course, has its own equivalent for the metaphor, but there are some basic distinctions that separate cinematic and literary metaphors.

In order to create the film metaphor, the film maker juxtaposes two concrete images in such a way as to imply that one thing is the other. To use a simple example, a film maker sets up a camera in front of a grammar school; he shows the children waiting nervously and impatiently for the eight o'clock bell to sound. When the bell rings he shows some of the children flowing into the corridors of the school. This footage would imply one meaning. The film maker then goes to the local stockyard, and this time films a flock of sheep lined up waiting to enter a slaughterhouse. This strip of film would imply another meaning. If the film maker splices these two strips of film together, creating a film metaphor, he forces his audience to consider in what ways the two shots are similar. The basic implication is that the children are sheep. Both children and sheep are herded about; both are being prepared for a market; the lives of both are subject to many pressures and influences over which they have no control; both have no freedom. In this instance, the viewer draws a conclusion on the basis of two images which have been dynamically opposed to each other.

This technique, however, is not necessarily the most desirable way to create a film metaphor, as Pier Paolo Pasolini has argued. A legitimate juxtaposition, he indicates, might be a comparison between a man (Gennarino) grinding his teeth, and a hyena with its teeth bared. But it "would be inconceivable to think of a film proceeding along these lines for a period of two solid hours, [while] in a novel, one could easily go on piling up metaphor after metaphor for two hundred pages." Pasolini goes on to suggest that the film maker actually creates the metaphor through innuendo, by forcing the images. That is, if the intention is to represent Gennarino as "having the characteristics of a hyena, he can show the image of Gennarino grinding his teeth in such a way that the viewer can form his own mental picture of the corresponding metaphor, i.e., the hyena, or if not exactly a hyena, then perhaps a panther or a jackal."[3]

John Howard Lawson, in his provocative study of audiovisual language and structure, *Film: The Creative Process*, gives an example of a film metaphor that was created by juxtaposing a seemingly unrelated sound track with a shot of a book.

In *Handwriting*, a nine-minute film by Charles Rittenhouse, the spoken text is a poem:

> Once I heard a white bird,
> I studied its speckled wings,
> I deciphered its markings.

On the screen, the poet is turning the pages of a book, and the pages are compared to the bird's wings, the print to its speckled markings. If the words were accompanied by shots of the white bird, the images might be beautiful, but their relationship to the words would be pedestrian and unnecessary: something new is created by the juxtaposition of the bird and the book.[2]

As Lawson suggests, Rittenhouse's metaphoric comparison possesses a quality of freshness and unpredictability. Initially, the viewer would probably be perplexed by the seemingly unrelated combination of the bird and the book, but he is sure to grasp the connection almost immediately. From that point on, he is able to derive both satisfaction and enjoyment in considering the correspondences between bird and book.

What most audiences would anticipate when they heard the poem's first line is a shot of a seagull skimming over the tops of the waves. This mundane association of word and image, however, would transform the experience into a sort of audiovisual cliché—i.e., the "poetic moment."

There are, of course, film clichés just as there are literary clichés—worn-out expressions like "green as grass," "a sickening thud," or "a clinging vine." Likewise, if a film maker manages to employ a shot or a film comparison that is particularly striking, there is sure to be a raft of imitators. For instance, at one point in the history of film, the sex act was portrayed on the screen by means of exploding fireworks, waves crashing over rocks, or flames leaping up in a fireplace. (And film makers today have not entirely deserted that technique; it reappears, for example, in Sidney Furie's *Lady Sings The Blues* [1972].) Similarly, passages of time would be handled by showing pages being blown off calendars, the hands of a clock spinning around, or verdant landscapes dissolving into "winter wonderlands." Today's films have spawned a whole new crop of clichés: the obligatory pot party; the couple in bed together naked from the shoulders upward; couples in love running in slow motion across parks, along the water's edge, or through meadows; violence in slow motion. . . . The film cliché, predictably, is an excellent index of an enfeebled imagination.

When the writer or the film maker uses a metaphor, the comparison between two things is implied. However, when a simile is used, the comparison is explicitly stated. In the previously cited example of a metaphor from *As You Like It*, Jaques' line read, "All the world's a stage." If that same line were altered to read, "All the world is like a stage" then the line would become a *simile*, for the comparison would be expressed by the word "like." Nearly every literary simile makes use of some connective word such as "like," "as," "than," or "resembles."

It is much more difficult to distinguish the film metaphor from the film simile, for film has no real equivalent for a connective word. Nevertheless, it could be argued that the two can be distinguished on the basis of emphasis. In literature, for example, the simile is less emphatic than a metaphor: "he is like a pig," as opposed to "he is a pig." Similarly, the film simile is less forceful than the film metaphor. For example, a camera might show an expensively dressed woman pacing back and forth in a chic apartment; the next shot shows a well-groomed Persian cat pacing back and forth in another part of the same room; the third shot cuts back to the woman again. The juxtaposition of these shots creates a film simile. Allying the cat with the woman does not suggest that they are identical; it merely implies that they are similar in some respects.

It is also possible for a film simile to occur within a single shot. A recent television commercial showed several owners grooming their dogs for a competition. What became readily apparent to the audience was the striking resemblances between the owners and their dogs. A heavy-set individual with large jowls was pictured grooming his bulldog and, next to him, a lean, delicate-looking greyhound was being positioned by a tall, thin, ascetic-looking man. The simile, in film, provides the artist with a means to comment obliquely upon a character or a situation; the simile, obviously, can also help a viewer discover an important aspect of a character that might otherwise go unnoticed.

Another, allied figure of speech that is sometimes adopted by the film maker is personification. In poetry as well as prose, personification occurs when an abstraction, an inanimate object, or something in nature is endowed with human characteristics. "Death sings a mournful tune" would be an example of an abstraction personified; "the highway calls the traveler" an instance of an inanimate object which had been personified; "the tree spread its arms out against the sky" an example of nature personified. When the artist uses personification, he demands that his audience identify the object or idea with a human being or at least a human characteristic. Personification in films is rare, but it does occur. The following four shots were taken from the screenplay of David Lean's film version of Charles Dickens' *Great Expectations* (1946):

4. MEDIUM CLOSE SHOT. Pip (a young boy) kneeling near
   tombstone. Wind gets louder. Pip looks around nervously
   towards the camera.

5. LONG SHOT. From Pip's eyeline of the leafless branches
   of a tree, which look to Pip like bony hands clutching
   at him.

6. MEDIUM CLOSE SHOT. Pip looks around as in #4.

7. MEDIUM SHOT. Of the trunk of an old tree from Pip's
   eyeline . . . The tree looks sinister to Pip like a
   distorted human body.[3]

In this particular scene, Lean's problem was to discover concrete correlatives for Pip's apprehension, and his solution was
to personify the branches as bony hands and the old tree as
a distorted human body. Ordinarily, the branches and trunk
of the tree would simply represent part of the context of a scene
but, because they are personified, they make a positive, meaningful contribution. More obvious examples of personification appear
in cartoons and animated films: animals assume the characteristics
of human beings; waves reach out, clutching at a foundering
boat; trains and cars are endowed with personalities. The use-
fulness of personification, for the writer as well as the film maker,
is its ability to suggest striking and unusual parallels between
man and his surroundings.

An even more suggestive associational device, however, is the
symbol. In Greek, the word *sumbolon* means "token for identification"; in Latin, *symbolum* means "sign" or "token." A sign
or a token is, in a sense, a kind of shorthand device. On the
highway, a diamond-shaped sign indicates to a driver that he
should reduce his speed; in mathematics, the sign $+$ indicates
that two quantities are to be added together. Through continued
use, both of these particular signs have come to have a fairly
explicit meaning. A symbol, like the sign or the token, also stands
for something, but it differs in that it is much more richly suggestive. The sign does not arouse emotions, but the symbol can.
Conventional symbols (symbols whose meanings are relatively
fixed through general agreement) are frequently the objects of
heated and passionate emotions: the Stars and Stripes, the cross,
the six-pointed star of Judaism represent some obvious examples.
In literature, a particular word may be employed so consistently
over a period of time that it attains the status of a conventional
symbol. This has happened with many words; the rose, for ex-

ample, has become synonymous with love, the snake with evil, and the nightingale with melancholy.

More frequently, however, the symbol does not have a fixed or generally accepted meaning. A single literary symbol can often be interpreted many different ways—and no particular interpretation is necessarily "right" or "wrong." Typically, the symbol is something that is concrete, i.e., it can be seen, smelled, heard, or touched. It is possible for a symbol to be an object, such as the red letter "A" that Hester Prynne wears on her blouse in Hawthorne's *The Scarlet Letter;* or a whale, as in Melville's *Moby Dick;* or perhaps a person, such as the anxious Joseph K. in Franz Kafka's *The Trial.* Had Kafka given Joseph a full name, his symbolic value would have been diminished, as a last name sets a person apart from his fellowmen. In the work, then, the artist usually gives an important symbol unusual stress or emphasis, often through repeated references to it. Most symbols, however, are characterized by a density, an air of mystery, and a variety of possible meanings.

In a film, the symbol functions precisely as it does in a literary work; it is concrete, often slightly mysterious, and highly suggestive. As in literature, symbols in film derive their meanings from the total context of the work. Orson Welles' highly acclaimed *Citizen Kane,* for example, makes extensive use of symbolism. One of the opening shots of the film shows the decayed elegance of Kane's immense estate, Xanadu. In the course of the film, the audience learns that Kane has spent much of his lifetime building and furnishing this contemporary palace —thus, Xanadu becomes a symbol for his ponderous yet empty "success." The snowflake paperweight and Kane's old sled, "Rosebud," come to symbolize the normal childhood that he was denied; the acres of *objets d'art* with which he surrounded himself are symbolic of the beauty that was so conspicuously absent in his own life.

In many instances, a film symbol may be developed over a period of time. The authors of *The Motion Picture and the Teaching of English* point out how a physical landscape, over a period of time, can attain symbolic meaning:

In Michelangelo Antonioni's *L'Avventura* (1960), the symbol of human alienation and loneliness comes not through a verbal image but through the whole first twenty-five minutes of pictures of people individually, or in pairs, picking their way along the jagged face of a great rock island in the Mediterranean, losing sight of each other, moving apparently aimlessly in what is a search for a girl who has disappeared from them, perhaps into the sea. The rocky surface, washed by a sea, is sharp as death and lovely as life—at one moment breathtaking in beauty and the next chilling in ferocity as it lashes the inlets where there is no chance for boat or man to come ashore safely.[4]

It is not uncommon for a film maker to use a landscape symbolically. In Hiroshi Teshigahara's *Woman in the Dunes* (1964), the ever-present, constantly shifting sand almost attains the status of a mute, yet extremely expressive character. Roman Polanski's *Cul-de-Sac* (1966) takes place in a castle that is separated from the shore by a slender causeway; surrounded by the sea, the castle is both a trap for its occupants and a perverse world in miniature. And anyone who has seen the harsh Scandinavian landscapes of Ingmar Bergman's films will find it very difficult not to view his settings in symbolic terms.

Frequently, a character in a film will emerge as a symbol. As in literature, such a character is usually ambiguously defined; his personality and characteristics tend to be emblematic or representative rather than highly individualized. In Federico Fellini's study of middle- and upper-class dissolution, *La Dolce Vita* (1959), there are two instances in which a very simple young country girl appears. Next to nothing is known about her, but in contrast to the other characters in the film, who are jaded, depraved, or both, the girl stands out as a symbol of innocence, honesty, and compassion. Sometimes a film maker will portray a character as a conventional symbol. In Ingmar Bergman's *The Seventh Seal* (1957), a stern, emaciated figure dressed in a black robe and cowl is the major antagonist. No one is surprised when he tells the film's protagonist, a knight named Antonious Block, that he is called Death.

The film symbol, like the literary symbol, can be relatively simple or extremely complicated, depending on the kind and quantity of meaning with which the artist has invested it. What is clear, however, is that the symbol demands from an audience an active involvement, with it and with the events that surround it. Ultimately, a member of the audience must determine for himself how a symbol is being used and what it represents.

A much simpler form of symbolism is allegory. The allegorical narrative tells a story beneath which there is yet another story. Most frequently, it will be found that the characters and events of the surface story correspond, usually in a one-to-one relationship, with characters and events of another time and place.

During the Middle Ages, the allegory flourished: *Piers Plowman, The Pearl,* and Chaucer's *Nun's Priest's Tale* are just a few examples of early allegorical narratives. In recent years, few writers have attempted allegorical fiction (in part, perhaps, because the success of an allegory is largely dependent on the reader's ability to recognize and follow the complex network of parallels—literary, social, religious, and so on—established by the author). One famous contemporary example, however, is George Orwell's *Animal Farm.* Here, the basis for the allegory was current political developments, which Orwell's readers were (and are) thoroughly familiar with; thus, his book was a great success. Superficially, Orwell appears to be telling a tale about a barnyard insurgency, but he is actually presenting a scathing indictment of the totalitarian state. As a result of the novella's popularity, *Animal Farm* was brought to the screen as a feature-length cartoon in 1955. More recently, John Barth has written a sprawling Rabelaisian novel entitled *Giles Goat-Boy.* In the novel, the world is presented as a gigantic university which has been divided into east campus and west campus. The parallels between the conditions of the contemporary world and Barth's university, between famous historical personages and the characters who populate the novel, are too striking to be overlooked.

The recent French film Z (1969), directed by Costa-Gavras, utilizes many of the techniques of allegory. The story line is relatively simple. A pacifist leader comes to a certain unnamed European country to speak; during his stay, he is assassinated, and a subsequent inquiry reveals that the assassination was encouraged, promoted, and defended by military leaders of the unnamed state. Even though no particular country or individual is ever named, it is impossible to ignore the obvious parallels of the events in Z to similar political situations in Greece, Spain, Czechoslovakia, Vietnam, and the United States.

In its most simple form, allegory involves dramatizing an idea by personifying the components of that idea. For example, in John Bunyan's famous seventeenth-century allegory *The Pilgrim's Progress,* a man named Christian journeys toward a place called

the Celestial City and along the way encounters characters such
as Mr. Worldly Wiseman and the Giant Despair. In creating his
Christian allegory, Bunyan renders concrete mental states and
concepts that are usually abstract (Despair, Doubt, Promise,
etc.). Likewise, in his dark, sardonic farce *Dr. Strangelove*
(1964), director Stanley Kubrick gives his characters such unlikely names as General Jack D. Ripper, Colonel Bat Guano,
Captain Mandrake, Chief of Staff "Buck" Turgidson, and President Merkin Muffley. (To say nothing of the ex-Nazi, Doktor
Wierdeliebe, who, after the fall of the Reich, has become a
prominent American scientist now called Dr. Strangelove.) In
both the literary and the film allegory, characters' names frequently indicate what the characters are meant to represent.
There are, of course, exceptions: William Golding's *Lord of the
Flies* (brought to the screen in 1963 by Peter Brook) is an
allegorical novel that does not use the names of the characters
in an obvious fashion.

When the writer or the film maker utilizes allegory as a form,
there is typically a discrepancy between what he appears to be
saying and what he is actually saying. The same thing occurs
when the artist, for the sake of freshness or emphasis, decides to
make use of overstatement (sometimes referred to as hyperbole)
or understatement.

For the artist, overstatement has a variety of uses: it can
produce a comic effect or a serious emphasis; or it may merely
be dramatically convincing, perhaps wildly fanciful. When Ten-
nyson, in his poem *The Eagle,* describes the bird as being "close
to the sun in lonely lands," he is making obvious use of overstatement, or hyperbole, for the reader knows that the earth is
actually some 93,000,000 miles from the sun. Yet the line is persuasive; it portrays the eagle as a tremendously powerful figure
that, from an immense height, seems to lord it over the vast
territory that lies beneath him. The reader accepts the exaggeration because it manages to get at those qualities that people of
all nations and times have admired in the eagle. Similarly, much
of the comedy of America's earlier films was heavily dependent
on the use of hyperbole or exaggeration. In Edward Cline's
Never Give a Sucker an Even Break (1941), the laconic W. C.
Fields offers to drive a woman, who he believes is about to
have a baby, to the local hospital. Fields speeds through the city

narrowly averting disaster at every street corner. Terrified at his driving, the woman passes out; Fields, believing that she is about to give birth, drives even faster. The subsequent trip to the hospital is madness itself: cars careen around corners at incredible speeds, pedestrians are nearly run over, there are a half-dozen minor collisions en route but, incredibly, no one is hurt. Similarly, an expression like "I'm so hungry I could eat shoe leather" is an instance of verbal hyperbole—but in the Chaplin masterpiece *The Gold Rush* (1925), there is a marvelous scene in which the tramp with great delicacy and ceremony literally proceeds to feast upon his shoe.

The opposite of hyperbole, of course, is understatement. Understatement derives its outrageous quality from the discrepancy between what the speaker is saying and his manner of saying it. Jonathan Swift, eighteenth-century satirist and master of understatement, once said, "Last week I saw a woman flayed, and you will hardly believe how much it altered her person for the worst." In *A Modest Proposal*, probably his best-known example of understatement, Swift assigns himself the role of a "reasonable" and dedicated citizen who is addressing himself to the problem of Irish overpopulation. By means of a perfectly logical argument, he proposes a method by which the "excess" infants of Ireland could be made "useful members of the commonwealth"; they should be slaughtered at an early age and served up as a national dish, the remainder to be shipped abroad as a delicacy, thus favorably augmenting the national treasury's balance of payments. Through understatement, Swift brilliantly conveys his point that, in effect, "the English are devouring the Irish."

Film, of course, can readily utilize understatement in dialogue, but such a use would represent a literary rather than a cinematic trope. Understatement in film involves a visual or aural discrepancy between what the audience is seeing and what they are being told.

Perhaps the audience is watching a mock-documentary on "Man's Progress." The narrator waxes eloquent over man's engineering triumphs and the audience witnesses brief shots of suspension bridges, gigantic dams, and an orbiting spaceship; the narrator then points out that man has made great strides in the field of medicine, and the screen shows some shots of an artificial limb, an X-ray machine, and a heart-transplant operation. The narrator continues to enumerate man's contributions to civilization. Then, suddenly, he intones, "Man's progress, of course, necessitates some small sacrifices," and the viewer sees entire cities shrouded in smog, beaches littered with broken bottles, beer cans, and papers, polluted streams and rivers, and thousands of cars jamming the arteries of a modern expressway. In relation to the appalling visuals, the audio represents a blatant example of understatement.

Although visual understatement can be utilized in many ways, it is most frequently employed in comedy. A character standing on the edge of a bridge announces to the world that he cannot swim and is going to take his own life. He leaps from the bridge, but lands in ankle-deep water. A would-be saboteur vows to blow up a building, but when he depresses the plunger of the detonator only a whiff of smoke and a barely audible explosion results. Understatement frequently relies upon a reversal of expectations; consequently, it is similar in nature to irony.

In literature, as in film, irony can take several forms: verbal irony, situational irony, and irony of fate. All ironies depend upon an incongruity of some sort: usually either a discrepancy between what is said and what is intended, or a discrepancy between what is expected and what actually happens.

Of the three ironies mentioned above, verbal irony is the closest to understatement; in fact, it is often very difficult to tell them apart. Verbal irony possesses a double-edged quality, it cuts two ways simultaneously. When Samuel Butler writes, "I would not be—not quite—so pure as you," he seems to be paying a compliment to the person he addresses, whereas he is actually doing just the opposite. In film, verbal irony is not entirely limited to dialogue. Wind and rain lashing a billboard that announces "Welcome to Florida, the Sunshine State" would be an obvious use.

Situational irony usually entails an event that produces just the opposite result of what the participants had anticipated. When Rosencrantz and Guildenstern accompany Hamlet to England bearing orders for Hamlet's execution, it is ironic that the two courtiers meet with the very fate that had been intended for Hamlet. Likewise, when Eve succumbs to the serpent's entreaties because she has been promised Godlike powers, it is ironic that she only succeeds in becoming mortal.

In David Lean's screen version of *The Bridge on the River Kwai* (1957), a British colonel (Alec Guinness) agrees to let his captured battalion construct a bridge for the Japanese because he feels the work will save their morale. It is ironic that he does manage to save their morale, but only by building a bridge that will obviously be used to transport enemy troops and munitions. And it is even more ironic that when the allied commandos arrive to destroy the bridge, which the colonel had hoped would stand for 600 years as a monument to British ingenuity and expertise, the colonel actually attempts to save it.

Irony of fate, or "cosmic irony" as it is sometimes called, operates on the assumption that fate is a force that actively intervenes in men's lives, almost always to their detriment. Although Oedipus is an overly proud and often arrogant man, he honestly attempts to avoid killing his father and marrying his mother. But Oedipus is a fated man, and no matter what he does he cannot elude his tragic destiny; in the course of the play, all the prophecies come true.

Vittorio De Sica's neo-realistic *The Bicycle Thief* (1948) appears to tacitly support the conventions of cosmic irony. A hopelessly poor Italian named Antonio has an opportunity to work as a billposter, but the job requires that he own a bicycle. After considerable sacrifice, he does manage to obtain the bicycle; then, on the very day he starts his new job, the bicycle is stolen. His attempts to regain the bicycle fail and, driven to desperation, he steals another, and is subsequently caught and humiliated. Like Oedipus, Antonio's life appears to be fated, and it seems as though there is nothing he can do to elude that fate.

Another instance of irony that occurs in both literature and film is ironic point of view: the discrepancy between what the characters say and do and what the writer or the film maker really means. This technique, often used satirically, permits the artist to mock his own creation. For example, W. H. Auden's poem *The Unknown Citizen* is supposedly a tribute by the State to the ideal representative citizen, but the tribute reveals the anonymous JS/07/M/378 (the name of the citizen) to be a mindless conformist who has lived a totally vacuous and passive existence. In Richard Attenborough's *Oh! What a Lovely War*, the British show girls, in an attempt to secure recruits from the audience, sing out "We don't want to lose you, but we think you ought to go." To the audience, it is patently obvious that the film's creators are satirizing the mindless chauvinism which the girls epitomize.

Because it makes use of apparent contradiction and inconsistency, paradox is somewhat allied to irony. In Greek *paradoxos* means "incredible; conflicting with expectations." A paradox is a statement that appears not to make sense. In one of his *Holy Sonnets* John Donne says:

> Batter my heart, three-personed God: for You
> As yet but knock, breathe, shine, and seek to mend:
> That I may rise and stand, O'erthrow me . . .

When Donne asks God to overthrow him so he "may rise and stand," he is employing a paradox. Literally, Donne's statement is self-contradictory, for to be overthrown is just the opposite of rising. The impact of Donne's paradox lies in its shock value: the contradiction forces the reader to reconsider the line. The key to the meaning of Donne's paradox lies in the word "rise." If rise is understood in the sense of spiritual rather than physical ascension, then the line makes perfectly good sense. Donne asks God to overthrow his proud spirit so that he can attain the humility necessary for salvation.

A film which has baffled many reviewers and critics because of its extensive use of enigma and paradox is a collaborative effort by avant-garde novelist Alain Robbe-Grillet and director Alain Resnais entitled *Last Year at Marienbad* (1961). In his introduction to the text of the film,[5] Robbe-Grillet suggests that the film's paradoxes are apparent rather than actual. By using an example of two people exchanging remarks, Robbe-Grillet argues that when people converse they actually exchange *views,* that is, they literally envision what they say. Hence, to Robbe-Grillet, there is no sharp line separating fantasy from reality; the image in the mind's eye is as real as the image of external reality. Thus, a sudden and seemingly paradoxical shift of place or the use of an enigmatic point of view is not a paradox at all, but merely a reflection of the mind's alternation between inner and external realities.

Allusion is another means by which both writers and film makers are able to enrich and intensify their narratives. Basically, an allusion is an indirect reference to something that lies outside the work itself; most frequently, the allusion refers to a historical personage or event, or some work of art. When the artist employs allusion, he allies his work to the emotions or ideas of another work. Although allusion represents a highly efficient method of communicating meaning, it is not entirely without risk, for the artist is assuming that his reader or viewer will be familiar with the event, person, or work to which he alludes. If the artist's assumption is correct, then a single line can greatly enlarge the resonance of his work; if, on the other hand, the allusion is too arcane or esoteric, then not only is the allusion lost on the reader or viewer, but it can easily confuse or disorient him as well.

As far as literature goes, most serious readers are familiar with the Bible and Shakespeare, and many with classical mythology as well. Thus, when William Blake, in *Song*, writes: "With sweet May dews my wings were wet/And Phoebus fir'd my vocal rage . . ." the reader recognizes that Phoebus is an allusion to Apollo, the Greek god of the sun. Or if a writer describes a character as being a "veritable Iago," the reader will immediately recall the diabolic evil of Othello's Ancient in Shakespeare's tragedy. On the other hand, few contemporary readers will recognize that a line in the drunken porter's speech in *Macbeth*, "Here's a farmer that hanged himself on the expectation of plenty," is an allusion to the abundant harvest of 1606 which was followed by a marked slump in the price of corn. Today, the same problem would hold true for a writer who referred to the Maharishi Mahesh Yogi. Most contemporary readers would be familiar with the onetime guru of the Beatles, but ten, or even five years from now, another reader would most likely scratch his head in amazement.

Films, certainly, can employ allusions in much the same way as literature. Godard's films, for instance, draw heavily from political and literary works; Marx, Engels, and Mao are cited in his *La Chinoise* (1967), Dostoevski and Pascal in *Pierrot le Fou* (1965). The world of art, as well, is often the source of allusions: Hitchcock refers to Michelangelo's *Pietà* in *Topaz* (1969), while Robert Altman alludes to Leonardo da Vinci's "The Last Supper" in *M*A*S*H* (1970), though to be fair, Buñuel had used the identical shot nine years earlier in *Viridiana*.

More importantly, though, seventy-five years of film making has provided the contemporary director with a rich source of

cinematic allusions. To the casual filmgoer, the following incident
in François Truffaut's *The Wild Child* (1970) is no more than a
little piece of comic business: a man peers into the nozzle of a
water hose, trying to discover why it refuses to work, and is
suddenly squirted in the face as the practical joker standing on
the hose in the background steps off it. To the student of film
history, however, this sight gag is an allusion to one of the first
films ever made, Louis Lumière's *L'Arroseur arosé* or "Watering
the Gardener" (1895). Similarly, in Claude Chabrol's *La Femme
Infidèle* (1969), the audience watches as a murderer attempts to
dispose of a weighted body in a desolate marsh; the body at first
refuses to sink, and for several agonizing moments floats half-
submerged on the surface of the water. The episode, of course,
represents a tribute to Hitchcock, who used a similar incident in
Psycho (1960) when a psychopathic killer disposed of a body
and car in a swamp-like pond. More recently, however, Stanley
Kubrick's *A Clockwork Orange* (1972) includes a brutal, sadistic
scene in which the protagonist, Alex, and his gang break into the
home of a writer, rape his wife, and then beat up the writer; while
he is tormenting the couple, Alex dances about the room and sings
lines from Gene Kelly and Stanley Donen's *Singin' in the Rain*
(1952). The striking incongruity between the cruelty and violence
of the *Clockwork* scene and most viewers' past associations with
the lighthearted '50s musical combine in a peculiarly macabre
fashion.

Figurative use of language enables the writer to state truths
that he cannot express through a literal use of language; the same,
of course, applies to a film maker's "figurative language" of images
and sounds. A figure is not only a means of seeing the world in
new and startling ways, but it can also involve us emotionally;
make the abstract concrete; or condense, and thereby enrich, the
narrative. By employing metaphor, simile, or personification, the
artist can force us to make striking and unusual comparisons; or
perhaps he aids us in seeing the commonplace in uncommon ways
by his use of hyperbole or understatement. Because of its vividness,
its richness, its density, figurative language represents an integral
and substantial aspect of the narrative experience both in the film
and in literature.

REFERENCES

1. Andrew Sarris, ed., *Interviews with Film Directors* (New York: Avon Books, 1967), p. 367.

2. Ibid., p. 370.

3. Ibid., p. 367.

4. John Howard Lawson, *Film: The Creative Process* (New York: Hill and Wang, 1967), p. 200.

5. Karel Reisz, *The Technique of Film Editing* (New York: Focal Press, 1966), p. 238.

6. Marion C. Sheridan, et al., *The Motion Picture and the Teaching of English* (New York: Appleton-Century-Crofts, 1965), pp. 6–7.

7. Alain Robbe-Grillet, *Last Year at Marienbad* (New York: Grove Press, 1962), p. 13.

In Arthur Penn's *Bonnie and Clyde* (1968), criminal violence is portrayed as high-spirited "fun" and common criminals are transformed into folk heroes.

Courtesy of Warner Bros., Warren Beatty, and Faye Dunaway

6

ANALYTICAL APPROACHES TO THE FILM:

CRITICISM

> All of us at <u>Cahiers</u> considered ourselves as future directors . . . while I was a critic I considered myself already a cinéaste. Today I still consider myself a critic, and, in a sense, I am one more than before. Instead of writing a critique, I direct a film.
>
> JEAN-LUC GODARD[1]

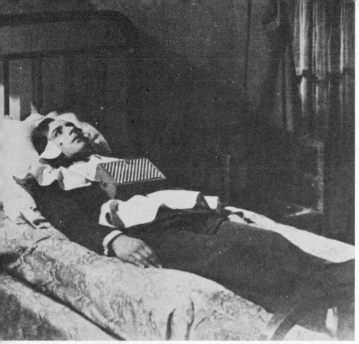

Here is a shot from what is probably the most famous surrealist film ever made, Salvador Dali and Luis Buñuel's *Un Chien Andalou* (1929).

Rarely has one man been so totally part of a film as Orson Welles was in *Citizen Kane* (1941), which he produced, directed, co-wrote, and starred in. Here, Kane (portrayed by Welles) marries his first wife (played by Ruth Warrick) on the White House Lawn.

Every Western made since 1903 is indebted, in some way, to Edwin S. Porter's ground-breaking "The Great Train Robbery."

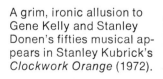

A grim, ironic allusion to Gene Kelly and Stanley Donen's fifties musical appears in Stanley Kubrick's *Clockwork Orange* (1972).

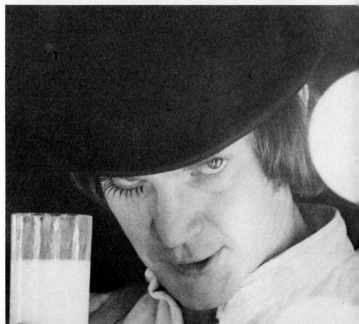

I N A GRIM, wry parable entitled "The Hunger Artist," Franz Kafka delineates with great skill the precarious and ironic position of the artist within society. Kafka's tale centers upon a man who is a professional faster, a man who voluntarily climbs into a small barred cage and refuses to eat for periods of up to forty days. The townspeople readily buy tickets for his performances, some even purchase season tickets. However, to insure that the hunger artist is kept honest, the townspeople appoint overseers. Early in the tale the narrator observes:

> Besides casual onlookers there were also relays of permanent watchers selected by the public, usually butchers, strangely enough, and it was their task to watch the hunger artist day and night, three of them at a time, in case he should have some secret recourse to nourishment.

In his brief reference to these "permanent watchers"—the butchers —Kafka is probably alluding to professional critics. These overseers, significantly, make no creative contributions themselves and even their roles are dependent on the faster's performances. In addition, since they are butchers by training, Kafka implies that critics are callous, insensitive mutilators.

This view of critics is not unusual. People generally tend to think of them in negative terms; they view critics as fault-finders, detractors, and censurers. And unquestionably, part of the critics' task is to make negative judgments when they seem appropriate. Yet there is another, more positive dimension to criticism, and it is this side which is most frequently slighted, if not overlooked entirely.

The critical attitude, for example, subsumes the following: the ability to ask and answer rational questions about a work of art; the ability to trace intellectual and emotional responses to specific features of the work; the ability to identify and evaluate the artist's purpose in any work.

But, in an even more fundamental way, it is frequently the critical attitude that spurs the artist to create in the first place. Novelist James Fenimore Cooper reportedly wrote *Precaution* in 1820 just to prove to his wife that he could write a better novel than the one they were currently reading. Similarly, film maker John Cassavetes (*Shadows* [1960], *Faces* [1968], *Husbands* [1969]), dissatisfied with films that were in his estimation too "thing oriented" or overly concerned with plot, turned to making his own films in order to create films that expressed more human qualities and dealt with more kinds of problems that confronted real people.[2]

Since at least part of an artist's skill is critical, it should not be surprising that a number of gifted writers and film makers have succeeded as critics as well as artists. Henry James, T. S. Eliot, and E. M. Forster wrote criticism as competently as they wrote literature. In the realm of film, V. I. Pudovkin's *Film Technique* and *Film Acting* were probably as influential as the films he made, and certainly the criticism and theoretical essays of Sergei Eisenstein (translated and collected by Jay Leyda in *Film Form* and *Film Sense*) exerted a far-reaching influence on the development of the silent and early sound film. Among contemporary directors, Lindsay Anderson, Peter Bogdanovich, Claude Chabrol, Jean-Luc Godard, Karel Reisz, Susan Sontag and François Truffaut have all come to film making after first serving as critics.

But even if the critical-creative nature of the artist is ignored, criticism still fulfills an important function. As film critic John Simon has suggested, criticism enables the artist to receive a serious response to his work; it also can direct us to a work's excellence; and finally, "To the extent that criticism can accelerate the verdict of the ages, it can speed up the coming of pleasure and enlightenment. . . ."[3]

It would be erroneous, however, to think of all critical writing on the film as being basically the same. Ezra Pound, in his *ABC of Reading*, distinguished between the six different classes of writers who created literature. Similarly, there appear to be four different classes of writers who create what is generally referred to as film criticism: the film reviewer, the film critic, the film scholar, and the film theorist.

These four categories, it should be noted, overlap in actual practice. For example, while most of Pauline Kael's contribution to *The Citizen Kane Book* could generally be described as film criticism, there are, in addition, many passages that represent clear-cut examples of film scholarship. Thus, the descriptions that follow discuss each of the four classes in a theoretical or "pure" sense.

Of all four categories, the work of the film reviewer is probably the most widely known. Usually, the reviewer is a staff member of a major metropolitan newspaper such as the *Los*

Angeles Times, or a columnist for a large-circulation, general-interest magazine like *New Yorker.* Reviewers as a category, however, are difficult to generalize about because of the enormous range of attitudes, intelligence, and sensibilities found within the group. Some reviewers, for example, restrict their favorable notices to "entertaining, family-style" films exclusively; and just about everyone is familiar with the reviewer whose sense of aesthetics is so contrary to our own that an unfavorable notice from him elevates the film to a "must see" for us.

Yet despite this range of differences, there are a number of traits that most reviewers share in common. In general, they do not look upon the film as an art form. Judith Crist, who is probably one of the most capable reviewers now working and who has written reviews for the New York *World Tribune,* the NBC *Today Show, TV Guide,* and *New York* magazine, has said:

> To me movies are very much a mass medium. I do not think that as a whole they can be regarded as an art form because most movies are not art . . . I have a very high tolerance for the commercial movie that doesn't pretend to be anything but a commercial movie. If it is well done. . . . I don't say that every single movie has to make a statement or anything. I do think that essentially all of us want to have a good time at the movies . . .[4]

Although Judith Crist is clearly suggesting that a film does not have to have a high or serious purpose to be considered, in her terms, "good," the criterion "a good time" could obviously preclude a number of important, perhaps disturbing or intellectually challenging films. Furthermore, to assume that film should not be regarded as art also seems questionable as this assumption, in essence, frees the reviewer from having to take the film seriously.

The reviewer, in addition, regards himself as performing something of a service to the community by functioning as a sort of early warning system. Again, to cite Judith Crist:

> I think the journalistic critic has very specific functions. . . . you must inform, basically, letting people know whether this is something they should or shouldn't see. . . . you have to let your "viewer" or reader—and you know who your reader is—know whether this is or isn't his cup of tea.[5]

Thus, a reviewer sees part of his or her task as prejudging the film for his readers; he tries to determine, beforehand, whether or not this is a film his readers should see.

Regarding the background that a reviewer should possess, Judith Crist suggests that in general "every possible thing you can experience helps. . . ." But a love of movies, wide viewing experience, a good liberal arts education, and some additional experience as a teacher, drama critic, and general reporter are some of the specific things an individual can do to prepare himself to become a reviewer.[6]

The critic, on the other hand, approaches the film with a somewhat different set of assumptions. On the question of whether or not film is art, John Simon, who has written film criticism for the *New Leader* and *Esquire,* has argued:

> . . . the first responsibility of the film critic is to recognize that there is, to be sure, a superficial difference between comedy and tragedy, and a profound one between good and bad, but that to view and review *all* films as anything but an art is at best trivial and at worst stupid . . . the point is that the critic . . . has no business considering entertainment as an end in itself, any more than he may consider art, in film or elsewhere, as something dreary and unentertaining. . . . And it is crucial to remember that there is no genuine entertainment without artistry, just as there can be no art that is unabsorbing, i.e. boring. There is, however, this proviso: artistry is not quite on the same level as art.[7]

The critic, then, approaches each film individually, always conscious that a film does possess the potential to be a work of art.

The task that the critic sets for himself is, once again, different from that of the reviewer. Pauline Kael defines it as follows:

> The role of the critic is to help people see what is in the work; what is in it that shouldn't be, what is not in it that could be. He is a good critic if he helps people understand more about the work than they could see for themselves; he is a great critic, if by his understanding and feeling for the work, by his passion, he can excite people so that they want to experience more of the art that is there, waiting to be seized. He is not necessarily a bad critic if he makes errors in judgment. (Infallible taste is inconceivable; what could it be measured against?) He is a bad critic if he

does not awaken the curiosity, enlarge the interests and understanding of his audience. The art of the critic is to transmit his
knowledge of and enthusiasm for art to others.[8]

Hence, while the reviewer is oriented toward judging the film,
the critic's primary interest lies in explicating the film. It should
also be pointed out that there are some critics who shun negative
criticism altogether. Jean-Luc Godard, in speaking of the film
critics at *Cahiers*, noted:

> . . . the thing that has always distinguished *Cahiers* from the rest
> is our principle of laudatory criticism: if you like a film, you write
> about it; if you don't like it, don't bother with tearing it to pieces.
> One need only stick to this principle.[9]

Furthermore, the background and training of the critic is
generally more specialized and rigorous than that of the reviewer.
John Simon, for instance, suggests that the critic should be
"conversant with cinematography, literature, acting techniques,
painting and sculpture (form and composition), music, dance
(film musicals), and in view of the generally poor subtitles, as
many foreign languages as possible."[10]

The reviewer, then, tends to regard the film as an entertainment, while the critic contends that some films are art. The critic
concentrates on explicating the artistry of the film, whereas the
reviewer, by and large, is much more inclined to summarize the
film and to judge its entertainment value. The reviewer often
feels that he resembles his readership, in that he assumes that
his own responses will probably be representative of those of
his audience. The critic, on the other hand, does not see himself as a Typical Viewer, and simply prefers to follow his own
bent and interests. The training of the critic, furthermore, tends
to be much more specialized than that of the reviewer.

Nonetheless, it would be a mistake to conclude that film
reviews are insignificant simply because they appear to make
lesser demands on their creators as well as their audiences. Certainly, this attitude would do great disservice to the articulate
and insightful reviews of individuals such as Renata Adler, James
Agee, Judith Crist, Pauline Kael, Stanley Kauffman, Dwight
MacDonald, and Andrew Sarris. More to the point would be to
recognize that the intentions as well as the audiences for these

two forms of critical writing vary greatly. Criticism, for instance, tends to be directed toward smaller, more specialized audiences, whose members, the critic can assume, possess some rudimentary knowledge of the film art. Reviewers, on the other hand, can assume nothing. Therefore their freedom to employ special terminology or to make filmic or literary references or allusions is severely curtailed.

If Judith Crist can be considered as representative of the film reviewer and John Simon of the film critic, then Siegfried Kracauer, the author of *From Caligari to Hitler* and *Theory of Film,* exemplifies the approach of the scholar.

While the critic usually restricts himself to explicating a specific film, or in some instances the films of a particular director, the task that the scholar sets for himself is typically much broader in scope. In *From Caligari to Hitler,* for example, Kracauer set out to demonstrate that the films produced in Germany from approximately 1918 until 1933 accurately reflected the collective psychological mentality of the German people at that particular point in time.

The scholar may also set out to challenge or refute a popularly held belief. In her controversial *The Citizen Kane Book,* for instance, Pauline Kael researched the background of Orson Welles' famous film, noted the contributions of individuals other than Welles, and concluded that much of the artistry of the film that is generally ascribed to Welles alone should actually be credited to scriptwriter Herman J. Mankiewicz and cameraman Gregg Toland.

In addition, the style of the scholar differs from the critic's in several ways: it tends, generally, to be more restrained in tone and more objective in treatment. Furthermore, because of the broader scope of his inquiry, the scholar is more apt to rely upon secondary sources than the critic. For instance, in John Russell Taylor's critical study of some key film makers of the sixties, *Cinema Eye, Cinema Ear,* a brief six-page bibliography is included, but no footnotes. Kracauer's *From Caligari to Hitler,* on the other hand, contains some fourteen pages of bibliographical references (in small type) and approximately 600 footnotes.

In contrast to the scholar and the critic, the film theorist's attention is focused on very different kinds of questions. The theorist's approach is essentially a philosophical one, that is, he is concerned with questions such as "the true nature of the film medium" or "the most filmic way to use film." (Arthur Lipsett's "Very Nice, Very Nice" [1960] or Michael Whitney's "Binary Bit Patterns" [1969], for instance, could only be realized as film, but "Occurrence at Owl Creek Bridge" is equally successful as both a film and a short story.) The work of the theorist, however, can be extremely important, for in his self-conscious analyses of film, he often discloses new ways in which film may be employed or even perceived.

Because the theorist frequently assumes a proselytizing role, his writings often seem evangelistic and didactic in tone. Dziga Vertov, a Soviet film maker and theorist who directed experimental documentaries and newsreels, argues ". . . I would just like to establish that all we have been doing in cinematography up till now was a 100% muddle and diametrically opposed to what we should have been doing . . ."[11] Eisenstein, in an essay entitled "A Dialectical Approach to Film Form," modestly announces that "*Montage* has been established by the Soviet film as the nerve of cinema"[12] as if to suggest that an artistic method was granted official approval by the entire Soviet film industry. Gene Youngblood, a contemporary theorist and author of the provocative *Expanded Cinema*, writes:

> It has taken more than seventy years for global man to come to terms with the cinematic medium, to liberate it from theatre and literature. We had to wait until our consciousness caught up with our technology. *But although the new cinema is the first and only true cinematic language,* it is still used as a recording instrument. The recorded subject, however, is not the objective external human condition but the filmmaker's consciousness, his perception and its process.[13] [Italics added.]

Youngblood, obviously, has strong convictions regarding the cinema of experimental film makers such as Jordan Belson, Stan Brakhage, and the Whitney family; their work, in his estimation, employs the only "true" language of cinema.

Rarely is the film maker thought of as embodying the attributes of critic, scholar, and theorist, but the film maker deficient in these areas would make films within rigid and narrowly circumscribed boundaries. The film maker who was not also a theorist, for instance, would be forced to make the same type of film over and over; lacking a sense of "what might be" he could only mechanically reproduce "what has been" or "what is." And the film maker who was not simultaneously a critic and a scholar would generally proceed without a sense of film history; as he was unaware of where the cinema had been, it would be nearly impossible for him to know where it had arrived.

Jean-Luc Godard, in an interview, explained the significance of a director possessing a critical and historical perspective:

> Criticism taught us to love Rouch and Eisenstein at the same time. To criticism we owe not excluding one aspect of the cinema in the name of another aspect of the cinema. We owe it also the possibility of making films with more distance and of knowing that if such and such thing has already been done it is useless to do it again. A young writer writing today knows that Molière and Shakespeare exist. We are the first cinéastes to know that Griffith exists. Even Carné, Delluc, or René Clair, when they made their first films, had no true critical or historical formation. Even Renoir had very little (it *is* true he had genius.)[14]

Godard's allusion to Molière and Shakespeare as examples of the literary yardsticks against which a young writer measures himself suggests that, for him, the writer's relationship to his work parallels the director's relationship to the completed film.

This view of the director's role was probably first fully articulated by François Truffaut when he, along with Godard and others, wrote film criticism for *Cahiers du Cinema*. Truffaut, in an article entitled "*Les Politiques des Auteurs*," outlined his concept of the director as *auteur*. In an interview some years later, Truffaut indicated that he still considered his theory valid:

> . . . the man who has the ideas must be the same man who makes the picture. This being so, I am also convinced that a film resembles the man who made it—even if he didn't choose the subject, didn't choose the actors, didn't exclusively direct them and let assistants do the editing—even such a film would . . . profoundly reflect in depth, for instance through the rhythm, the pacing, the man who made it . . . .[15]

The ideal *auteur*, of course, would be the individual with a personal vision who could exert complete artistic control over his films.

In general, the *auteur* concept placed a high premium on the identifiably personal qualities of individual film makers. This emphasis on the personal led the critics at *Cahiers* to be "for" some directors and "against" others. In the United States, this tendency was carried one step further by *Village Voice* film critic, Andrew Sarris, who ranked fourteen directors under a category entitled "Pantheon Directors" and delegated nearly 200 other directors to categories ranging from "The Far Side of Paradise" to "Miscellany" (see Sarris' book, *The American Cinema*).

The *auteur* theory met with considerable resistance, especially from film critic Pauline Kael, who in an essay entitled "Circles and Squares, Joys and Sarris" argues that the *auteur* theory was not only rigid but virtually incomprehensible. The *auteur* advocates, for instance, argued that there was no such thing as a good or bad film, but only good and bad directors. Thus, ran the argument, the worst film of a good director would hold more interest than the best film of a bad director. Given this premise, Pantheon director Alfred Hitchcock's *Marnie* (1964) would be deemed more "interesting" than the *Maltese Falcon* (1942) by the then unknown John Huston.

Pauline Kael also contended that the *auteur* theory gave rise to pompous and overblown praise of inconsequential films. Referring to *auteur* criticism, she wrote:

> If they are men of feeling and intelligence, isn't it time for them to be a little ashamed of their "detailed criticism" of movies like [Otto Preminger's] *River of No Return* (1954)?[16]

In her extensive analysis of Orson Welles' *Citizen Kane*, Pauline Kael offered her own view of the director's role:

> The director should be in control not because he is the sole creative intelligence but because only if he is in control can he liberate and utilize the talents of his co-workers who languish (as directors do) in studio-factory productions. The best interpretation to put on it when a director says that a movie is totally his is not that he did it all himself but that he wasn't interfered with, that he made the choices and the ultimate decisions, that the whole thing isn't an unhappy compromise for which no one is responsible; not that he was the sole creator but almost the reverse—that he was free to use all the best ideas offered him.[17]

Thus, a director is not unlike a symphony conductor: even though the score may not be his, he still imposes his own interpretation on the music through his direction of the individual members of the orchestra. Yet, at the same time, he must depend upon these individual musicians, to varying degrees, for the successful realization of a particular performance. In much the same way, the film director must rely upon his writer, cameraman, editor, and actors to transfer his vision intact to one long strip of celluloid.

Virtually any commercial film—for that matter, any experimental film—passes through a number of different stages of development, revision, and refinement. When the film is finally completed or "in the can," it possesses an autonomous existence of its own, a life apart from the film's creator and his intentions. Thus, though the director may have had very specific goals in mind when he made the film and perhaps had even articulated these intentions publicly, it is important to realize that having completed his artistic task, the film's creator—like everyone else— now exists apart from the work.

The essence of this precept is contained in a statement attributed to the English novelist, poet, and critic, D. H. Lawrence. "Trust the tale, not the teller," warned Lawrence. In other words, there may be a discrepancy between what the artist set out to do and what he actually accomplished. As a corollary, the artist's conception or understanding of his own work does not exhaust its possibilities. Hence, like a universe in miniature, a film demands its own life, and must ultimately be dealt with on the basis of its own premises, images, sounds, and rhythms. Certainly, any successful attempt to assess or comprehend a film must proceed from this basis.

Furthermore, the notion that there is *one* way to understand a film must also be discarded. There are, it may be argued, as many different ways to comprehend a film as there are points of view —although this is not to say that all the varying points of view are equally valid critically.

Some years ago, René Wellek and Austin Warren undertook an exhaustive analysis of literary criticism entitled *Theory of Literature*. In their analysis of the different types of critical approaches to literature, they noted that most criticsm fell within one of two major categories: *extrinsic criticism*, which dealt with

literature primarily as a social document or as a direct manifesta-
tion of the author's personality; and *intrinsic criticism*, which
concentrated on analysis, description, interpretation, or, sometimes, special areas of concern such as genre.

It seems to me that most of the critical approaches described
by Wellek and Warren are, with some revisions, equally applicable to the study of film. Thus, using *Theory of Literature* as a
guide, what follows is a discussion of eight separate critical
approaches to the film.

Film and History

Working from the assumption that film makers as well as their
audiences are products of a specific historical period and environment, some critics have argued that films should be studied as a
means of better understanding the mentality and mores of a
society at an earlier historical period. Siegfried Kracauer, for
example, contends:

> The films of a nation reflect its mentality in a more direct way
> than other artistic media for two reasons: first, films are never the
> product of an individual. . . . Second, films address themselves,
> and appeal to the anonymous multitude. Popular films—or, to be
> more precise, popular screen motifs—can therefore be supposed
> to satisfy existing mass desires.[18]

One illustration of Kracauer's second point might be the cheerful,
optimistic American films that flourished during the Depression
years, films such as Busby Berkeley's *Golddiggers of 1935* (1935),
Gregory La Cava's *My Man Godfrey* (1936), Frank Capra's *You
Can't Take It With You* (1938), and Howard Hawkes' *Bringing
Up Baby* (1938). These films—which showed life as most people
wished it could be—were a striking contrast to the gray reality of
the real world. In his *Short History of the Movies*, Gerald Mast
suggests:

> If the conventional studio films displayed any consistent per-
> sonality, it was one that reflected the general moral assumptions
> and human values of the era as a whole rather than that of any
> individual director. Inherent in almost all the films was the view

that the sincere, the sensitive, the human would inevitably triumph over the hypocritical, the callous, the chaos of social machinery. American movie audiences, escaping from the realities of the Depression outside the movie theater, ran inside it to see human grit triumph over suffering and human kindness triumph over financial, political, and moral chicanery. If the optimism of Hollywood films provided the audiences with the tranquilizer it needed it also strengthened its audience's belief that eventually good people would make bad times better.[19]

Similarly, Edward Mapp in his *Blacks in American Films: Today and Yesterday* is employing an extrinsic approach when he traces the portrayal of the black in American films. Mapp's survey ranges from the various film versions of *Uncle Tom's Cabin* (there were four: 1909, 1914, 1918, and 1927) and D. W. Griffith's *The Birth of a Nation* (which primarily employed whites in blackface) up to and including the black machismo films of the early '70s: Gordon Parks' *Shaft* (1970), Gordon Parks' Jr.'s *Super-Fly* (1971). At least until the '60s, the portrayal of the black in American films was severely limited. Mapp cites Lawrence Reddick's list of black stereotypes:

1. The savage African
2. The happy slave
3. The devoted servant
4. The corrupt politician
5. The irresponsible citizen
6. The petty thief
7. The social delinquent
8. The vicious criminal
9. The sexual superman
10. The superior athlete
11. The unhappy non-white
12. The natural-born cook
13. The natural-born musician
14. The perfect entertainer
15. The superstitious churchgoer
16. The chicken and watermelon eater
17. The razor and knife "toter"
18. The uninhibited expressionist
19. The mental inferior[20]

The extrinsic approach is also useful, of course, for the writer who wishes to study the changing film portrayal of sexual mores, the military, religion, women, the American Indian, scientists, homosexuals, or for that matter, any identifiable social class, role, or phenomenon.

Studies such as Mapp's invariably improve our comprehension of longstanding social patterns; however, certain problems arise when one attempts to extrapolate from the basic facts. There is no way, for example, of proving how these portrayals of black Americans affected the individuals who watched these films, even though it would be fair to guess that most of the films were highly influential simply because of the large numbers of people who saw them.

What, too, of the film maker's role? Does it seem likely, as Gerald Mast suggests, that the film maker functions as a sort of social barometer, sensing what the public wants and giving it to them? Or would it be more accurate to conclude that the film maker's vision is so unique and powerful that it actually alters the sensibilities of large numbers of people?

Some critics, for instance, have suggested that the enormous popular success of *The Sound of Music* (1965) was a direct consequence of the film's deliberate exploitation of saccharine sentimentalism. Dwight MacDonald, writing for *Esquire*, remarked that he was genuinely surprised that the film didn't win all the Academy Awards that year (it received ten nominations and five awards) since it had literally everything going for it: nuns, for vivid camera material; children, for cuteness; family drama, TV style, for wholesomeness; Nazis for villainy; and picturesque shots of Salzberg's baroque architecture, beautiful countryside, and the peasants' quaint costumes for atmosphere.[21]

On the other hand, the film maker whose films contain sentiments and ideas that are not popularly held invariably meets with hostility. For example, when Luis Buñuel's *L'Age d'Or* (*The Golden Age*) opened in 1930 at Studio 28 in Paris:

> . . . the *camelots du roi* and other Catholic and Fascist gangs threw brimming inkpots at the screen and slashed paintings by Dali, Ernst, and Tanguy exhibited in the lobby. The right wing press egged the gangs on and howled against Buñuel. Finally, Police Commissioner Chiape had the film banned.[22]

By contrast, today—over three decades later—*L'Age d'Or* is critically acclaimed and is a favorite viewing choice of many film societies, colleges, and universities. On the other hand, most films of that same period—well-received in their own day—have now been consigned to oblivion. The fact that *L'Age d'Or* is no longer an *objet du scandale* indicates a clear shift in public opinion over the years. It would be tempting to argue that the film itself may have been partly responsible for that shift, but once again, this type of conclusion is impossible to prove.

While studies of particular films often yield valuable insights into the sociological milieu of certain periods, it is also true that it is sometimes necessary to study the cultural context of certain films in order to avoid erroneous or anachronistic judgments. This type of approach, of course, is still within the purview of extrinsic criticism.

For example, given Eisenstein's Marxist orientation, it is not surprising that he would produce a film such as *Potemkin*: it portrays the czarists as callous, insensitive puppets and features a virile, sympathetic proletariat as the collective hero. *Ivan the Terrible* (1944), however, presents a basically sympathetic portrait of an individual who employed harsh, sometimes tyrannical tactics in his political machinations. In order to understand how Ivan fits into the canon of Eisenstein's work, it is necessary to know that Ivan, a sixteenth-century autocrat, destroyed the power of the Boyars and thus was able to unify the Russian principalities into one czardom. Thus, for Eisenstein, Ivan was instrumental in leading Russia toward the nationalist state it finally achieved in the twentieth century.

Not only is it informative to investigate the context surrounding a historical figure in a film, but sometimes it is instructive to compare the film's version of that individual with other accounts—often, there are discrepancies. The real-life Clyde Barrow and Bonnie Parker, for example, were a far cry from the sympathetic creations of Arthur Penn in *Bonnie and Clyde*.

Sometimes, rather than portraying an actual historical figure, a characterization may simply be modeled after a real person. Willie Stark, in Robert Rossen's film version of Robert Penn Warren's *All the King's Men* (1950), was based upon Huey Long, governor and U.S. Senator from Louisiana. An even more famous example, of course, is Orson Welles' *Citizen Kane*, in which Kane is modeled after William Randolph Hearst.

Examining the differences between the historical model and the fictional counterpart should not be undertaken simply to dutifully record deviations from the original, but rather to gain a more accurate understanding of an artistic response to historical circumstances. The essay that follows is an example of

extrinsic criticism. Charles Higham compares the wealthy pub-
lisher, William Randolph Hearst, to Welles' fictional creation,
Charles Foster Kane.

CITIZEN KANE AND CITIZEN HEARST
Charles Higham

One crucial question we must ask ourselves about *Kane* is:
does the film accurately reflect William Randolph Hearst's life?
Welles has in recent years continued to insist that Kane was not
Hearst. He told the *New York Herald Tribune* (September 11,
1951):

He was a great figure. I didn't have a battle with him. He had one
with me. *Citizen Kane* was *not* an exposé of Hearst as everyone believes. I didn't make a picture about him.

Hearst was raised by his mother. He had a very happy childhood.
My man Kane was raised by a bank. That's the whole point of the
picture. They were different types of men. For example, my man Kane
would never have fought me the way Hearst did. Instead, he would
probably have offered me a job.

Hearst and the people around him did me terrible harm after the
picture appeared. Some day when I write my autobiography I'll tell of
the damage that they did me, and the frame-ups they tried.

The big similarity between Hearst and Kane is that both of them
had no responsibility to the people. But in spite of everything I hold
no malice towards him. I don't see why anyone should hold any malice
toward him.

We must admit, first, that the portrait is a caricature, and that
the picture of Hearst's relationship with his mistress, Marion
Davies, is not intended to be literal: her devotion to Hearst was
absolute, and his death came to her as a bitter blow.* The real
Hearst was capable of love, and life at San Simeon, his fabled
ranch in California, sparkled in its heyday with a brightness and
gaiety contradictory to the squalid luxury of Kane's ranch picnic
and the echoing, tomb-like emptiness of Xanadu.

---

*Others have taken a grimmer view, hinting at homosexuality and other per-
versions and suggesting that Marion Davies was often kept a virtual prisoner at
San Simeon. We will probably never know the truth, but I have preferred the
more charitable view.

In other respects, the film follows Hearst's career with mixed fidelity. The plot adjustments are significant. Both Hearst and Kane were only children, born in 1863, and both were expelled from Harvard. Hearst's father and mother were not, like Kane's, poverty-stricken boardinghouse keepers. George Hearst was a well-to-do farmer's son, whose silver strike at the Comstock Lode made him a millionaire, and whose later interest in the Homestake Mine still further increased his massive fortune; he became a senator and earned a respected place in the American Dictionary of Biography. In the film these parents are left a deed to the Colorado Lode by a defaulting boarder, Fred Grange, and the Kane fortune is thus founded not by the acumen and push of a paternal figure but by blind chance.

Hearst's love for his mother is echoed in Kane's love for his, and the Rosebud image—symbol of a lost childhood and the protection of a mother—is an apt reflection of the fact that Hearst was forever haunted by the memory of the charming, tender, and noble Phoebe Hearst.

The origin of the character of Susan Alexander Kane* has usually been attributed to Marion Davies alone, and the portrait is indeed visually based on her: the nervous doll's face, the aureole of blonde hair, the chirrupy voice. It is true, too, that through his Cosmopolitan Pictures outfit, first in New York and then in California, and by purchasing a major shareholding interest in MGM (and later Warner Brothers) Hearst secured for her a career in the cinema which she really didn't want, and was embarrassed to see applauded by every Hearst newspaper critic who valued his job. In fact, a stronger foundation of the character is in Sybil Sanderson, Hearst's first love, an opera singer whose initial American appearance at the Met was applauded in an exorbitantly large article in Hearst's *San Francisco Examiner* (prototype of Kane's *Inquirer*); for her the infatuated Massenet composed *Thaïs* and *Manon*—the mode of the former appropriately and perfectly parodied in Herrmann's *Salammbô* excerpts. Sybil Sanderson died ruined by drink and ill-health in her late thirties, her career dogged by scandals. Although Hearst's wife, Milicent Wilson, was a dancer and not, like Emily Monroe Norton, the niece of the president, much of her personality is echoed in the gentle, staid, and unexciting Emily.

---

*Rita Alexander was the name of Welles's screenplay typist.

Politically, the parallels with Hearst are often startlingly close, for instance in reference to *The Inquirer* having started the Spanish-American War.

Hearst bought the New York *Morning Journal* in 1895; it was originally an unsuccessful paper, and he changed it into a one-cent sheet of a popular type. He raided the New York *World* for members of Joseph Pulitzer's staff. The combination of sensationalism and jingoism elevated the circulation to 1,506,000 copies. He attacked President McKinley (as Kane attacked President Monroe), and provoked war with Spain. Later came the Chicago *American*, paralleling the Chicago paper for which Leland worked. During the Depression, he sold or scrapped papers, like Kane.

The famous exchange of telegrams between Hearst and Frederic Remington, an artist whom he sent to sketch the Spanish butchery in 1896, is reproduced almost intact in the script. When Remington cabled the *Journal*, "Everything quiet. There is no trouble here. There will be no more. I wish to return." Hearst replied: "Please remain. You furnish the pictures; I'll furnish the war." Later, Hearst published a Remington drawing of a Cuban girl stripped for searching by Cuban soldiers: the rival newspaper, the *World*, managed to produce the girl herself, who confessed she had been searched under conditions of privacy by matrons, and that Remington could not have drawn her.

Once the film closely echoes an actual conversation: the remark Kane makes to Walter Parks Thatcher when the banker complains that the newspapers are losing a million dollars a year —"I'll have to close this place—in sixty years." This is directly drawn from Phoebe Hearst's comment upon learning that her son's *Examiner* and *Journal* were losing the same amount: "At that rate, he could last thirty years." Bernstein is based on two of Hearst's associates, Arthur Brisbane and S. S. Carvalho, and Jedediah Leland is based on John Francis Neylan, the Irish lawyer and political reporter who fought gallantly against graft and became Hearst's counsel and lawyer for the Hearst empire: a man of probity, he was often thought of as Hearst's conscience, and he is heartlessly parodied in the figure of the sophomoric, verbose, and often foolish figure presented on the screen.* There are parallels, too, in the character of Jim W. Gettys with Boss Charles F. Murphy, a political manipulator who opposed Hearst at the time Hearst ran for governor of New York; Thatcher is a caricature of

---

*Leland's dismissal for his unfavorable notice of Susan Kane's operatic debut echoes Hearst's sacking of many for similar "mistakes."

J. P. Morgan. Kane's politics authentically echo Hearst's: Hearst began as a Jeffersonian democrat, using *The San Francisco Examiner* as a radical organ to fight political corruption, big business, and monopolies, while at the same time deeply involved in business ventures of his own. Later, he became fascist, exploiting a fascist potentiality in the lower middle class, a class that had once been as Jeffersonian as he was.

As Raymond Gram Swing wrote in his *Forerunners of American Fascism:* "During the lifetime and power of this single man, the entire economic fabric was made anew. We see in him the beginning of the modern era, hear through him the social outcry against it, and find him today, no longer a rebel, but resigned to it and accepting its fascist implications."* Kane's speeches in the film echo Hearst's, and also Hearst's letters—like the famous one written in 1906 to Arthur Brisbane and quoted by W. A. Swanberg in his definitive *Citizen Hearst:*

> We still maintain a republican form of government, but who has control of the primaries that nominate the candidate? The corporations have. Who control the conventions? The corporations. Who own the bosses and the elected officials? Are they representatives of the people or the corporations? . . . If the corporations do all this—and they surely do—can we any longer maintain that this is government for the people?**

In his campaign for the governorship of New York, expertly condensed and parodied in the film, Hearst promised "government ownership" to restore to the people "everything the corporations have stolen from them." Later, when Hearst's Americanism—like Kane's—changed its meaning he began to admire Hitler and Mussolini. In the mid-thirties, after he had established his fascist stand and had visited Hitler, Hearst attacked the communist menace. So the changes were rung and the film mockingly rings them too.

And *Kane's* final conclusion is the same as Swanberg's, finishing his life of Hearst on a series of question marks. Studying that life, Swanberg wrote, was for most of his contemporaries "as confusing as adding two and two and discovering for once that it did not make four." Swanberg concludes that Hearst would have been dangerous in high office and that his rejection by the voters was a fine proof of the democratic system.

*Julian Messner, 1935.
**New York, Charles Scribner's Sons, 1961.

He had integrity, on occasion. He had principles and beliefs which he firmly swore by at any given time but which could fluctuate as wildly as a compass near the pole. His crippling weakness was instability, vacillation, his inability to anchor his thinking to a few basic, rocklike truths that were immovable in his heart. . . . For all his potency of utterance, he seemed a creature of caprice, lacking real substance.

(In some ways an appropriate comment on the worst side of Welles himself.) Swanberg adds that Hearst was "unrivaled in the magnificence of his failure, the scope of his defeats, the size and scope of his disappointments." The film exactly captures this quality of magnificent catastrophe in a style not dissimilar to that which characterized Hearst's journalism—as Swanberg says, "Combining elements of the peep-show, the Grand Guignol and the foghorn." Welles's achievement was to blend those elements into art. As Swanberg says: "Who but Citizen Hearst would have set himself up as a king, owned seven castles, fought for the common man, looted the world of art, squired a bevy of actresses through Europe?" The answer is no one. And who but Orson Welles, the explosive *Wunderkind* of American radio, theater, and film, could have brought his life to the screen? No one again. One is left only with the wish that Welles had drawn his own conclusions about this friend of the working man, the Jeffersonian, the fascist, the master of empires, instead of leaving us with an enigma as baffling as a great stone Easter Island face.

Film and Ideas

Luis Buñuel first attracted critical attention with "Un Chien Andalou" (An Andalusian Dog"), a film he made with Salvador Dali in 1929. During a recent interview, Buñuel admitted that his reading of Freud, the Marquis de Sade, Marx and Engles, and entomologist Jean Henri Fabre had a definite influence on his early work.[23] "Andalusian Dog," which Buñuel says was inspired by psychoanalysis, opens with a startling scene of a woman's eyeball being sliced open by a razor blade and goes on to unfold a series of vivid, illogical, dreamlike scenes. And while "Andalusian Dog" reveals an inner world, *Los Olvidados* (1950) presents a vivid and moving portrait of Mexico City's economically destitute, though characteristically Buñuel refrains from moralizing over the inequities that produced this poverty. The point, however, is that the artist's exposure to ideas does affect his work;

philosophy, science, and theology are frequently the conceptual starting points for a film.

Polish director Roman Polanski once said that an early experimental film of his, "Two Men and a Wardrobe" (1958), was the only film he had ever made that "meant something." The film, he noted, was "about the intolerance of society toward someone who is different."[24] Polanski, of course, was not suggesting that all his other films meant nothing. Rather, he was admitting that this particular film *originated* from a conviction about the nature of society.

Similarly, in *Modern Times* (1936), Chaplin advances the idea that mechanization has a dehumanizing effect on man. In Fellini's *La Dolce Vita* (1959), the idea that the upper echelons of Italian society are characterized by decadence, boredom, and frustration predominates throughout. Stanley Kubrick once stated that in *2001: A Space Odyssey* (1968) he was attempting to realize a scientific definition of God.

Films, of course, are capable of dealing with virtually any idea, but generally ideas in narrative films tend to fall in one of four major categories: films which deal with questions of fate and involve issues such as freedom and necessity (De Sica's *The Bicycle Thief* [1948]); films which center on religious questions such as the existence of God, the divinity of Christ, and the nature of salvation (Bergman's *Winter Light* [1961]); films which are concerned with man's relationship to nature (Flaherty's *Nanook of the North* [1920]); and the largest category— the condition of man—which includes: man and family (Ray's *The World of Apu* [1959]); man and society (Welles' *The Trial* [1962]); man and the state (Rossen's *All the King's Men* [1948], Costa-Gavras' *Z* [1969]); man's conception of love (Curtiz' *Casablanca* [1942], Widerberg's *Elvira Madigan* [1967]); and man's conception of death (Kurosawa's *Ikiru* [1952], Bergman's *Cries and Whispers* [1973]).

Some years ago, it was not unusual for films to open with prefaces or prologues that pointed up the central idea or ideas of the film (both Buñuel's *L'Age d'Or* and his *Los Olvidados*, for instance, had prologues, although both were gross oversimplifications of the films). In a few instances, films would have afterwords which often explained what happened to certain characters after the resolution of the basic conflict (this format is still retained by the television series *The FBI*). Today's audiences, however, tend to consider prefaces and afterwords superfluous.

In some films the characters themselves often serve as important vehicles for ideas. In Stanley Kubrick's *Dr. Strangelove*, Group Captain Mandrake's position as a British exchange officer, and therefore an outsider, gives him a relatively detached point of view; he functions much like a *raisonneur* or "voice of reason." Thus, we share in his incredulity when U.S. officer Bat Guano refuses to let him smash open a coke machine to get change to call the President about the crisis on the SAC base. Whereas Mandrake typifies the use of a spokesman figure to communicate ideas, Guano himself is used to stand for a particular idea: he represents the one-track reactionary mind, the mentality that becomes so obsessed with certain entrenched values, such as the sanctity of private property, that he can neither see nor understand anything else, regardless of the circumstances.

Sometimes, the sum total of the speeches and actions of characters in a film can stand for large-scale ideas. Peter Brooks' screen version of William Golding's *Lord of the Flies* opens with a somewhat Edenic note: following an emergency plane landing, presumably somewhere in the Caribbean, a group of English choir boys are forced to take refuge on a lush tropical island. Two of the boys, Ralph and Piggy, attempt to establish an orderly, parliamentary method of dealing with their situation. They are frequently opposed, however, by Jack, who begins advocating the practices of savages. Another boy, a loner named Simon, goes off into the jungle by himself and ends up mystically communing with the severed head of a wild pig. Ralph and Piggy, then, come to be associated with many of the desirable features of civilization: reason, order, nonviolence; Jack and his followers, on the other hand, consistently display barbaric traits: passion, ritual, and aggression; and Simon, the mystic, is allied with religion.

A film maker can also express his ideas by means of a suggestive pattern of metaphors and images. In Antonioni's *Zabriskie Point* (1970), for example, the plot is loosely structured around a bizarre plane theft by a young anarchist, but most of the film is devoted to a critical examination of American society. The title of the film is derived from a particularly desolate stretch of desert in Southern California, reportedly the lowest point in the United States. Antonioni uses the desert as a metaphor for the arid and soulless materialism that stigmatizes much of America's value system. Throughout the film, Antonioni's camera dwells on the bleak iconography of the American landscape: the gigantic, grotesquely illustrated billboards; promotion campaigns for plastic, look-alike suburban developments; camper-equipped tourists who swarm through national parks like a plague of locusts; mammoth and impersonal office buildings of steel and glass that dominate city skylines. Taken together, the metaphors and images of *Zabriskie Point* suggest that America, peopled by greedy and rapacious individuals, has become a vast wasteland. The film ends with a young woman fantasizing the destruction of an expensive desert retreat occupied by a group of businessmen and some real estate developers; this image merges with a second fantasy involving the destruction of a host of material goods: a well-stocked refrigerator, a rack of clothes, a tier of books, and so on. This slow-motion sequence clearly calls for the annihilation of both the materialists and the objects they covet.

All other things being equal, the film of ideas tends to be more interesting and satisfying if the ideas are mature and provocative. However, it should be pointed out that even if a film does express ideas that are banal, naive, or ignorant, the film itself may still be considered good, perhaps even great. D. W. Griffith's *The Birth of a Nation*, for example, is awkwardly burdened with excessive sentimentality and racism, but because of the superb technique that Griffith employed to unfold his narrative, *The Birth of a Nation* is generally considered one of the masterworks of the cinema.

Films, in other words, are not dramatized philosophy. Rather, they possess their own aims and justifications. In great films, ideas are often subordinated in order to achieve artistic unity. Dwight MacDonald, for example, was genuinely angered at critics who faulted Fellini's *8½* for lacking "solid intellectual content." Addressing himself to these critics, MacDonald wrote:

> Because it is technically sophisticated, and because it deals with major areas of experience, these critics look for philosophical depths in a movie which is superficial—I think deliberately—in every way except as a work of art.[25]

Thus, the critic's search for ideas should not make him oblivious to the film's other values. And finally, the critic should be cautious of assuming that the ideas expressed in a film are systematically held by the film's creator. Obviously, a communist could make a film that sympathetically portrays a capitalist hero and vice versa.

Film and Biography

With certain films—especially the films cited in *auteur* criticism—it is clear that the individual most responsible for the look, shape, and feel of the final product is the director. From this premise—the director as cause—it would appear to follow that a knowledge of the director's life and personality can help in illuminating his work. For instance, knowing that Federico Fellini was once a caricaturist who worked around Rome's restaurants before he became a film maker helps to explain, at least in part, the broadly drawn caricatures of humanity that appear in his films so often. Similarly, the fact that Ingmar Bergman's father was a pastor obviously has some bearing on the religious questions that tend to dominate many of his early films. And it is fairly well known that the life of the young boy, Antoine Doinel, in *The 400 Blows* (1958) closely parallels in many respects the childhood of the film's director, François Truffaut. (" . . . [It] is neither optimistic nor pessimistic. . . . it is rather a personal testimony concerning a precise period of one's life," said Truffaut.[26])

Directors themselves often indirectly encourage this biographical approach by producing films that bear remarkable similarities to their own lives. Fellini's *8½*, for example, deals with a film director experiencing a series of personal, artistic, and professional crises; a more recent effort of his, *Fellini Roma* (1972), retains that same strong autobiographical flavor.

A film maker who consciously seeks to display his own unique personality in his work is a subjective film maker. *The 400 Blows* and *8½*, then, would be considered creations of subjective film makers. In this sense, Alfred Hitchcock might appear to represent another example of the subjective film maker. Hitchcock, for instance, appears physically in a minor part in nearly all of his films, and he possesses a style of film making so personal and idiosyncratic that Truffaut considers him "one of the few film makers on the horizon today whose screen signature can be identified as soon as the picture begins."[27] Yet, despite his readily identifiable style, Hitchcock's films reveal little or nothing about his personal life. Following a fifty-hour interview with Hitchcock, Truffaut concluded that there was a "striking contrast between Hitchcock's public image and his real self."[28] Thus, Hitchcock is really representative of the objective film maker, the director who effaces his own personality, or takes refuge behind a persona or mask in order to disguise that personality.

Though it is true that the biographical approach can serve to illuminate certain features of the film, it is not clear that the approach accomplishes much more. For instance, one need not know a director's biography before his work can be understood. After all, it is not self-evident that our understanding of Shakespeare suffers greatly because we know so little about his personal life.

Furthermore, it is simply wrong to assume that there *must* be a direct cause-and-effect relationship between the director's private life and his work. One need not be depressed in order to create tragedy, nor happy to create comedy. Art, certainly, is something more than a mere transcript of life; the artist who is unwilling to alter reality in order to enhance his art is probably not much of an artist to begin with.

A study of a film maker's life, therefore, can help to bring about a better understanding of his milieu and the influences which shaped him, but this approach should not replace a careful analysis of the work itself. Ultimately, it is the work that justifies our interest in the man, not the other way around.

Extrinsic criticism nearly always relates the film to something that is outside the film itself: how a film reflects a historical period, how a film embodies ideas, or how a film reflects the personality of its creator. Intrinsic criticism, on the other hand, confines itself almost exclusively to the film itself and concentrates on areas such as description, analysis, interpretation, and evaluation.

Imagery

Of all the distinguishable artistic qualities of a film, one of the most important is its use of visual images. The kinds of images that a film maker employs are, of course, directly related to the size of his canvas. Large-scale narratives such as David Lean's *Lawrence of Arabia* and *Doctor Zhivago* (1966), for instance, are dominated by sweeping panoramic shots that may contain as many as a thousand individuals. Ingmar Bergman, on the other hand, rarely deals with more than a half-dozen characters and frequently limits the settings of his films as well (*Cries and Whispers,* for example, centers around four women and takes place, almost exclusively, in three or four rooms). Bergman's subjects, in other words, require more probing, intimate kinds of images, while the epic-like proportions of Lean's narratives produce images much broader in scope, and much less personal.

Generally, films possess major and secondary images. Secondary images, of course, are necessary for the development of the narrative but are not of themselves especially important. Major images, on the other hand, often call attention to themselves by their striking or unusual qualities. For example, anyone who has seen *Bonnie and Clyde* is not likely to forget the slow-motion, rag-doll dance of death toward the end of that film.

Furthermore, major images will often appear at important points of the narrative or in key scenes; the opening of *Patton,* for example, with the larger-than-life figure of Patton in the foreground and the huge American flag in the background establishes in the audience an attitude toward the controversial general that lasts the entire film. The mystery and ambiguity of the freeze frame that concludes *The 400 Blows* also impresses itself vividly upon the memory. Sometimes, major images are repeated throughout the film so that they function as a filmic leitmotif; the image of the woman—the Eternal Mother—rocking the cradle in Griffith's *Intolerance* and the accompanying subtitle serve to unify the film's four stories by suggesting that the same passions, joys, and sorrows that have affected people throughout history have remained basically unchanged.

Discussions of images in films should generally concentrate on the specific properties of individual images. How, for example, is the image lighted? Strong sidelighting, dividing a face into half dark, half light, may suggest that a character is divided against himself. Even the nature of the film stock should not be ignored: the grainy texture of John Cassavetes' *Faces* (1968) gives that film an authentic *cinéma vérité* look. Sometimes, specific colors or tones seem to dominate a film. For example, the yellows, golds, browns, and ochres of Bernardo Bertolucci's *The Last Tango in Paris* (1973) impart a sensuous earthy quality to the film. Camera angles, the distance from the subject to the camera, and even camera movements should be carefully noted; the restless, probing tracking shots of Alain Resnais in *Last Year at Marienbad* lend the film a decidedly impersonal, detached quality.

The purpose of undertaking a study of film imagery is to demonstrate that imagery is related, both literally and figuratively, to the overall meanings of a film. The opening dream sequence of Fellini's *8½*, for example, shows the film's protagonist, Guido, trapped inside an automobile in a traffic jam. It is an intolerable state and to worsen matters, the people in the cars around him stare impassively at him as he attempts to extricate himself from the car. Finally, he imagines himself floating up into the sky, away from the problems of earth, but almost immediately his foot is lassoed by a business associate and he is pulled back to earth. The implications of these images are fairly clear: the protagonist feels trapped, wants to escape, but is constantly being brought back to reality and its attendant responsibilities by other people.

The most dominant form of imagery in films is, of course, visual. Sound, however, makes substantial contributions to most films; thus, studies of a film's auditory imagery are also important areas of investigation. And even though films can only suggest the sense of smell, touch, taste, and movement, they can often create persuasive illusions. In Alfred Hitchcock's *Vertigo* (1958), for instance, the viewpoint character, Scottie Ferguson, experiences dizziness whenever he attempts to climb heights. In one crucial scene, Scottie is pursuing a woman up the steps inside a church steeple and has an attack of vertigo. Hitchcock wanted to show how the perspective would look from Scottie's viewpoint, and accomplished this by building a model of the stairway, laying it on its side, and combining a track-out with a forward zoom. The effect is very convincing.

Setting, Mood, and Atmosphere

For many people a setting is nothing more than a backdrop against which a narrative is played out; for them, what's important are the characters and what happens to them. In the

James Bond films, for example, the settings are invariably picturesque and exotic but they are not really integral to the narrative. That is, the same story could be told with a totally different setting without substantially altering the story. Change the island setting of *Lord of the Flies* to a mainland, however, and the story disintegrates: the primitive environment and the isolation are absolutely necessary to that narrative. Similarly, much of the impact of Bo Widerberg's *Elvira Madigan* would be substantially changed if the same story was set in the city rather than the country. Sixten, a Swedish count, has deserted the army, and Elvira, a tightrope artiste, has fled her stepparents' care. In the eye of society, their behavior is "unnatural," for they have committed legal as well as sumptuary transgressions; in addition, they are unmarried and living together. In the city they would surely be apprehended. In the country, however, the naturalness of their surroundings with its Rousseauist implications reinforces the naturalness of their love for each other. Despite the fact that ultimately, their love is doomed, for a brief period of time they share an intense, almost idyllic relationship.

In some instances, a setting might represent what T. S. Eliot once termed an "objective correlative." In his essay "Hamlet and His Problems," Eliot defines an objective correlative as a means of expressing an emotion, when "a set of objects, a situation, a chain of events" become the "formula of that *particular* emotion; such that when the external facts, which must terminate in sensory experience, are given, the emotion is immediately evoked."[29] In other words, a film maker might use a specific setting in order to evoke a specific emotional response. One example, discussed earlier, would be Antonioni's use of the desert in *Zabriskie Point* as an objective correlative for the arid emptiness of certain American values. In Fellini's *8½*, the steaming hot baths at the health spa are employed as an objective correlative for hell.

Some settings function as visual counterparts to states of mind or states of being. In Poe's "The Fall of the House of Usher" the description of the crumbling Usher mansion with its "eye-like windows" and the "barely discernible fissure" extending from the roof to the ground is, in fact, a portrait of its inhabitant, Roderick Usher. Similarly, the progressive deterioration of the Ambersons' mansion in Orson Welles' *The Magnificent Ambersons* (1942) parallels the decline of the Amberson family and the genteel and more leisurely way of life that they represented.

Settings can not only be employed so that they function as metaphors or symbols, but sometimes they may serve to provide a film's basic organization. Dennis Hopper's *Easy Rider* (1969), for instance, is essentially episodic in structure; the entire film is actually a series of episodes loosely organized around the motorcycle journey from Los Angeles to New Orleans. The order of the episodes could probably be rearranged, that is, some incidents could take place in an order other than the present one, but the west to east organization would have to be retained because it provides the film with most of its structure.

Studies of a film's setting usually concentrate on locale and include any physical properties that might be significant. Studies of mood and atmosphere, of course, include not only the setting, but lighting, camera angles, visual characteristics of the color or black and white film stock, types of lenses used, and any other notable special effects. Low key lighting and underlight, for instance, make substantial atmospheric contributions to most horror films. In *The Last Picture Show* Peter Bogdanovich chose black and white because he felt that it would be more evocative of the '50s—a decade during which most films were made in black and white—than color. The long-lens photography and the muted, impressionistic use of color in *Elvira Madigan*, on the other hand, make a substantial contribution to the romantic aura that surrounds much of that film. And in Fellini's 8½, when young Guido is caught by the priests during his visit to the huge prostitute Saraghina, the humor is enhanced by the use of fast-motion photography.

For the reasons given above, a study of the metaphoric function of the setting—its relationship to the central characters and thematic concerns of the film—will often help clarify the film maker's intent. It should be noted, however, that some films lend themselves to this type of critical approach better than others. Realistic or naturalistic films, such as Rosselini's *Rome: Open City* (1945) or more recently Troell's *The Emigrants* (1972), are primarily concerned with showing the world "as it is." Thus, settings tend to be employed to achieve verisimilitude rather than to suggest figurative meanings.

Style

If three film makers were each asked to produce a film from the same script, the finished works would probably be significantly different from each other in many respects. Each director would present the story in a manner reflecting his own individual style; thus, the differences in the films could not be accounted for by the subject matter. Stylistics, then, is the study of the way an artist handles his material, as opposed to its substance or content.

In general, there are three major types of stylistic studies: first, those dealing with the personal idiosyncracies of expression which identify the unique characteristics of an individual film maker; second, those dealing with a particular technique of expression; and finally, those that undertake to describe a harmonious fusion of the personal with the universal.

The first category, personal idiosyncracy, is perhaps the easiest to analyze. Some film makers, for example, have evolved film styles so unique and personal that it is possible to recognize their signatures without actually seeing the opening credits. The style of Federico Fellini is an excellent example. He favors, for instance, actors and actresses who have striking or unusual faces; his films often blend reality with fantasy in strange, unexpected ways; often the circus or the sea is used as a symbolic landscape; typically, he employs the same kind of music in many of his films; and with few exceptions, he essentially focuses upon the upward or downward moral progression of his protagonists.

Many other film makers also possess highly individualized styles: Sergei Eisenstein, Luis Buñuel, Alfred Hitchcock, Orson Welles, Ingmar Bergman, François Truffaut, Michelangelo Antonioni, and Jean-Luc Godard are just a few who come immediately to mind. Relatively few directors, however, have a style as pronounced, or "mannered," as those named above.

Sometimes, a film maker's style will be affected—at least in part—by the type of film he is making. For example, every western made since Edwin S. Porter's "The Great Train Robbery" flashed on the screen in 1903 owes something to the conventions and characteristic conflicts of that genre. It is difficult to imagine the western without the sweeping panoramic shots, a chase, the inevitable shoot-out, and so on. Thus, the style of any director attempting a western is partially dictated by the form. For instance, even movies as far apart in tone and sensibility as *Butch Cassidy and the Sundance Kid* and *The Wild Bunch* share certain features in common: the unspoken code of honor that binds outlaws to each other; the modernization of the West, which in turn is transforming the simple outlaw into an anachronism; the flight from civilization and the inability of the outlaw to adjust himself to his changing world.

The third category, the fusion of the personal with the universal, is a little more difficult to explain. In essence, the film maker's method of handling a particular shot or scene is stylistically identifiable as being uniquely his own, but the scene simultaneously possesses a universal quality as well. In Fellini's 8½, the final scene takes place at the movie set of the launching pad where all the people in the protagonist's life, both living and dead, real and imagined, join together in one great parade of humanity. The music, the striking collection of unusual individuals, the fantastical set of the launching pad, and the circus atmosphere of the scene combine in a way that strikes us as uniquely Felliniesque, yet the "parade of humanity" and the way that the scene slowly fades out in darkness convey a universal meaning that reaches beyond individual, temporal, and geographical limitations.

A stylistic analysis, in the broadest sense, includes all the artistic elements of a film. However, inasmuch as a film is essentially an organization of images, sounds, and movements, visual imagery might be a good starting point. Under this heading, the following factors should be considered as aspects of the film's overall style: camera angle and the distance from the subject to the camera (exaggerated angles often imply attitudes toward the subject); lighting (an important index of mood as exemplified in many of the dimly lighted and heavily shadowed early films of Ingmar Bergman); and the particular hue and character of color (Fellini, for instance, sometimes abandons conventional color tones as he did during Encolpius' journey across the open fields in *Fellini Satyricon* [1970] in order to impart a mythic dimension to the film). Furthermore, color can also be used symbolically, as in Antonioni's *Red Desert* and Bergman's *Cries and Whispers*.

Composition, which includes the arrangement of shapes, the predominance of horizontal and vertical lines, and the emphasis on angular or rounded forms, certainly falls within the realm of stylistic analysis. Though it is nearly impossible to discuss compositional values without reference to the film's content, it is generally true that angular shapes tend to be more visually disturbing than rounded ones; this is because of the general associations rounded forms call up (moon, sand dunes, faces) as opposed to associations with angular shapes (lightning, mountains, and most weapons). The harsh jutting angles in Robert Wiene's classic horror film, *The Cabinet of Dr. Caligari* (1919), for instance, serve to heighten the film's prevailing sense of tension and unreality.

The director's choice of filmic transitions also represents an important aspect of his film's style. Dissolves or fade-ins and fade-outs often impart a fluid, languorous rhythm to a film while jump-cuts and flash-forwards create the opposite effect. Similarly, the various techniques of camera movements—panning, tracking, dollying, zooming (an apparent rather than actual movement)—all impart their own special flavor to the film's style.

Any sort of characteristic optical distortion should be noted. The film maker's unique use of telephoto, wide-angle, or special-effect lenses such as the "fish-eye" may impart an unusual quality to the film's visual style.

Another major element of any stylistic analysis is the use of sound. Generally, there are five major areas of sound in film to consider: the sheer amount and intensity of sound; the interrelationship between dialogue and background sound; the use of a musical score; musical motifs; and any special or unorthodox use of sound.

Loud noises are often used to suggest pandemonium (the chariot scene in William Wyler's *Ben-Hur* [1959], for example) or even madness. Absence of sound—silence—can also be used to suggest madness or unbalanced states of mind. The near-silence of the opening dream sequence of Fellini's 8½, in which Guido finds himself trapped in an automobile in the midst of a traffic jam, serves to underwrite the desperate nature of his predicament; in the middle of a traffic jam, noise is normal while near-silence is abnormal.

Often it will be found that dialogue interacts with background noise to form a single mosaic of meaning. In Antonioni's *Red Desert* (1963), there is a particularly poignant scene in which Monica Vitti buys a partially eaten sandwich from an incredulous factory worker. While this human but somehow pathetic exchange takes place, the viewer sees in the background a factory with a monstrous exhaust stack which periodically spews out flames. The noisy "whoosh" of the fire combines with the muted conversation in the foreground to lend a peculiar intensity to the scene.

Music, which played an active role during the days of the silent film, is today even more intimately related to style. Music, for instance, can be used to establish certain moods or to help re-create a period, as in Peter Bogdanovich's *The Last Picture Show* (1971), where the popular songs of the '50s are used to recall that particular decade. Music can also serve as an ironic counterpoint to a film's visual imagery. Arne Sucksdorff's highly acclaimed short film "A Divided World" (1948) opens with the civilized and dignified music of Bach, but what the viewer soon sees are wild animals hunting and preying upon one another in a deadly contest of survival. As mentioned above, some film makers demonstrate a continuing preference for specific kinds music (Bergman's use of Bach, Fellini's choice of melodic circuslike tunes); in some cases, the association of the music with the narrative can be so strong that a few bars of the score may evoke the entire film for the viewer.

In some films, music may also be employed in such a way that a few notes of a musical score may actually function as a motif (a repetitive device which vividly recalls an earlier event and the context surrounding it). In Fritz Lang's *M* (1931), for instance, Peter Lorre plays a child murderer named Franz Becker. While wandering the streets in search of victims, Becker has the habit of nervously whistling a few bars from Grieg; after a short period of time, of course, the music becomes associated with the killer and even though the audience does not actually see Becker, the sound of the whistling signals his presence and evokes apprehension.

Unorthodox or unusual uses of sound should be carefully noted, for often they make important stylistic contributions. In Robert Enrico's "Occurrence at Owl Creek Bridge," for example, the rope being used to hang the protagonist snaps, he plunges into the water underneath the bridge, and, after disencumbering himself from his bonds, he resurfaces moments later a few feet downstream from where he had originally fallen. At this point, the voices of the Union soldiers on the bridge and the sounds of their footsteps are heard at a slower-than-normal sound speed (the effect is similar to hearing a 33⅓-rpm record being played at 16 rpm). The implication of this "slowing down"—which is occurring visually as well—is that time, in the conventional sense, has been stretched out or elongated. On the other hand, the eerie, haunting sounds that dominate the sound track of Jordan Belson's experimental film "Allures" (1961) were intended, according to Belson, to evoke a sense of the mystery of outer space.

Visual imagery and the use of sound, of course, constitute the two major areas in an analysis of style. But the writer should consider the following areas as well: characteristic conflicts or themes (does the film maker appear to be concerned with similar issues or conflicts in most of his films?); the form of the film (is it, for instance, a theatrical film, and if so, what type: western, melodrama, thriller? and how has the film maker contributed to or departed from the form?); the contributions of the individual actors and actresses; the settings of the film (are they used figuratively? are there prevailing patterns of movement throughout the film? that is, does the film seem to be dominated by vertical or horizontal images . . . are there images which suggest elevation? decline?); the film's tone (can you identify and describe it?). The matter of tone is an important consideration, for it usually reveals the film maker's attitude toward his subject.

Probably the most popular stylistic study is the analysis of the style of a specific director (sometimes known as a "monograph"). Typically, it concentrates on the individualizing touches that reveal the imprint of the director's personality, and it will often demonstrate that similar themes, symbols, and images are common to all of his films. Stylistic studies of a particular type of film—a genre—are not uncommon either. This type of stylistic analysis, however, generally passes over the unique and ideosyncratic characteristics of individual films and directorial styles in order to concentrate on the traits that are shared by all films of that same genre. Less common, however, is the stylistic study which concentrates on a single film. This study, generally, tends to be much more detailed than the two other examples and seeks to prove neither directorial consistency nor uniformity of genre patterns.

Through analysis of style, a writer can often identify what it is that sets film apart from other arts. Therefore, this kind of analysis represents an important critical approach. If there is any danger in the stylistic study, it is that in isolating the traits and characteristics of a particular film or group of films the writer may be tempted to place undue emphasis on "originality" or idiosyncratic touches, and thus overlook the significance of the film as a whole.

Evaluation

Of the various intrinsic approaches, it is perhaps the evaluative study that demands the most from the critic. Rather than explicating specific features of the film or a group of films, the critic must pass judgment on the work in its entirety; in addition, he must also be able to consider how the film relates historically, philosophically, and aesthetically to other important or great films.

Dwight MacDonald, film critic for *Partisan Review* and *Esquire* for many years, once listed some of the guidelines that he personally used to evaluate films:

> Are all the characters consistent, and in fact are there characters at all?
>
> Is it true to life?
>
> Is the photography cliché, or is it adapted to the particular film and therefore original?
>
> Do the parts go together; do they add up to something; is there a rhythm established so that there is form, shape, climax, building up tension and exploding it?
>
> Is there a mind behind it; is there a feeling that a single intelligence has imposed his own view on the material? . . .
>
> Did it change the way you look at things?
>
> Did you find more (or less) in it the second, third, nth time?
>
> How did it stand up over the years, after one or more "periods" of cinematic history had elapsed?[30]

MacDonald emphasizes, however, that these guidelines are not inflexible. Many films he admires are not strictly "true to life," among them Griffith's *Broken Blossoms* (1919), Marcel Carne's *Children of Paradise* (1945), Jean Vigo's *Zéro de Conduite* (1933), Wiene's *Cabinet of Dr. Caligari* (1919), Clive Brook's *On Approval* (1944), and Eisenstein's *Ivan the Terrible* (1944). And some films he considers great have no "characters" per se: Eisenstein's *Potemkin* (1926), Resnais' *Marienbad,* and Leni Riefenstahl's *Olympia* (1940).

Another question that the critic should consider in his evaluation is: Does the film deal with significant and perennial conflicts of human existence, or is it restricted to superficial and topical issues? In other words, does the film reach beyond the limitations of its specific language and culture to touch upon universal problems? An East African could not identify with the distinctively American rituals and conflicts involved in Mike Nichols' *The Graduate,* any more than we could understand a drama based on the institutions of his culture. By contrast, a film such as Satayajit Ray's *The World of Apu* has a much broader relevance, touching on the crucial events common to all human life: love, birth, death, the painful acquisition of self-knowledge. The characters and setting happen to be Indian, but that is incidental to the film's universality; the Bengali family Ray shows us could be any family, anywhere.

Films, in addition, can appeal to their audiences in different ways. Susan Sontag, in an essay entitled "Spiritual Style in the films of Robert Bresson," writes:

> Some art aims directly at arousing the feelings: some art appeals to the feelings through the route of the intelligence. There is art that involves, that creates empathy. There is art that detaches, that provokes reflection.[31]

In other words, a film such as Resnais' *Last Year at Marienbad,* which deliberately keeps its audience at a distance and concerns itself exclusively with formal structure—the "surfaces" of people, things and events—is not to be evaluated in the same way as De Sica's *The Bicycle Thief,* a film which arouses strong feelings of empathy and pity for the poverty-stricken and ill-fated protagonist, Antonio. Thus, when Pauline Kael attacks *Marienbad* by saying "The people we see have no warmth, no humor or pain, no backgrounds or past, no point of contact with living creatures, so who cares about their past or future, or their present?"[32] she is, in essence, insisting that the film deal with characterization in a traditional causal and sequential manner. Alain Robbe-Grillet, who wrote the script for *Marienbad*, argues that the spectator who tries to reconstitute some "Cartesian schema" will find the film difficult if not incomprehensible, but

> . . . the spectator [who lets] himself be carried along by the extraordinary images in front of him, by the actors' voices, by the sound track, by the music, by the rhythm of the cutting, by the passion of the characters. . . . the film will seem the most realistic, the truest, the one that best corresponds to his daily emotional life, as soon as he agrees to abandon ready-made ideas, psychological analysis, more or less clumsy systems of interpretation which machine-made fiction or films grind out for him *ad nauseam*, and which are the worst kinds of abstractions.[33]

Finally, the critic who writes an evaluation is also obligated to assess any moral, social, or philosophical conclusions that a film might advance or infer. The editor of *Encountering Directors*, Charles Thomas Samuels, attacked Arthur Penn's *Bonnie and Clyde* for its "cynical falsity" soon after the film was released. In a recent interview, Samuels pointed out that Penn deliberately causes the audience to empathize with the Barrows, then portrays their criminal acts as fun, while at the same time the activities of the police are characterized as cruel and psychotic. When the criminals are shot, Samuels noted, they bleed, whereas the lawmen do not; that tells you whose side the director is on.

Francis Ford Coppola's screen version of Mario Puzo's *The Godfather* (1972) perpetuates similar moral distortions. For instance, the portrayal of the Mafia patriarch, Don Vito Corleone, is extremely sympathetic: he is represented as a just, honorable man who is forced into violence by circumstances of poverty and self-preservation. And early in the film, when the undertaker, Amerigo Bonasera, sees the case against the two young men who had attacked his daughter dismissed from court, the implication is that "true" justice can't be obtained from courts of law; Don Corleone, however, settles the score with old-fashioned eye-for-an-eye, tooth-for-a-tooth justice. In other words, whenever violence or murder is perpetuated by the Corleones, their motivations (e.g., defending the life of a member of the immediate family, or avenging the murder of a sweetheart or brother) are nearly unimpeachable. What the audience never sees, however, are those occasions when the Mafia employs political pressure to ruin honest law enforcement officials, or applies force to intimidate the small, independent businessman who won't "play along," or uses murder to stop the crusading newspaper editor "who's out to make trouble." These omissions are in essence immoral, for they distort and lie about the real nature of people like the Corleones.

The evaluative essay, then, takes a stand. It speaks positively (or negatively) of the film's accomplishments (or failures) and forces the critic to assess the film on a variety of levels: originality, beauty, harmony, and profundity. All critical writing, of course, requires some degree of evaluation, but in the evaluative essay, arriving at a clear judgment of the film's worth as an entity is the critic's primary objective.

At the outset of this discussion of intrinsic criticism, it was noted that intrinsic criticism, essentially, concentrates on such areas as description, analysis, and evaluation. The following essay, "The Organic Structure of *Potemkin*," written by the director of that film, Sergei Eisenstein, describes the film's organizational pattern and points up some literary devices that Eisenstein was able to translate into a film form. Thus, the essay represents an example of intrinsic criticism and combines the techniques of description with analysis.

THE ORGANIC STRUCTURE OF POTEMKIN
Sergei Eisenstein

Potemkin looks like a chronicle (or newsreel) of an event, but it functions as a drama.

The secret of this lies in the fact that the chronicle pace of the event is fitted to a severely tragic composition. And furthermore, to tragic composition in its most canonic form—the five-act tragedy. Events, regarded almost as naked facts, are broken into five tragic acts, the facts being selected and arranged in sequence so that they answer the demands set by classical tragedy: a third act quite distinct from the second, a fifth distinct from the first, and so on.

The utility in the choice of a five-act structure in particular for this tragedy was, of course, by no means accidental, but was the result of prolonged natural selection—but we need not go into this history here. Enough that for the basis of our drama we took a structure that had been particularly tested by the centuries. This was further emphasized by the individual titling of each "act."* Here, in condensation, are the contents of the five acts:

Part I—"Men and Maggots." Exposition of the action. Milieu of the battleship. Maggoty meat. Discontent ferments among the sailors.

Part II—"Drama on the Quarterdeck." "All hands on deck!" Refusal of the wormy soup. Scene with the tarpaulin. "Brothers!" Refusal to fire. Mutiny. Revenge on the officers.

Part III—"Appeal from the Dead." Mist. The body of Vakulinchuk is brought into Odessa port. Mourning over the body. Indignation. Demonstration. Raising the red flag.

Part IV—"The Odessa Steps." Fraternization of shore and battleship. Yawls with provisions. Shooting on the Odessa steps. The battleship fires on the "generals' staff."

Part V—"Meeting the Squadron." Night of expectation. Meeting the squadron. Engines. "Brothers!" The squadron refuses to fire. The battleship passes victoriously through the squadron.

In the action of its episodes each part of the drama is totally unlike the others, but piercing and, as it were, cementing them, there is a repeat.

In "Drama on the Quarterdeck," a tiny group of rebelling sailors (a small particle of the battleship) cries "Brothers!" as they face the guns of the firing squad. And the guns are lowered. The whole organism of the battleship joins them.

In "Meeting the Squadron," the whole rebellious battleship (a small particle of the fleet) throws the same cry of "Brothers!" towards the guns of the flagship, pointed towards the *Potemkin.* And the guns are lowered: the whole organism of the fleet has joined them.

From a tiny cellular organism of the battleship to the organism of the entire battleship; from a tiny cellular organism of the fleet to the organism of the whole fleet—thus flies through the theme the revolutionary feeling of brotherhood. And this is repeated in the structure of the work containing this theme—brotherhood and revolution.

Over the heads of the battleship's commanders, over the heads of the admirals of the tzar's fleet, and finally over the heads of the foreign censors, rushes the whole film with its fraternal "Hurrah!" just as within the film the feeling of brotherhood flies from the

---

*When *Potemkin* was exhibited outside the Soviet Union, these part-titles were invariably removed by the various adaptors; the only foreign prints of *Potemkin* restored to its original form are those circulated by the Museum of Modern Art Film Library.—EDITOR.

rebellious battleship over the sea to the shore. The organic-ness of the film, born in the cell within the film, not only moves and expands throughout the film as a whole, but appears far beyond its physical limits—in the public and historical fate of the same film.

Thematically and emotionally this would, perhaps, be sufficient in speaking of organic-ness, but let us be formally more severe.

Look intently into the structure of the work.

In its five acts, tied with the general thematic line of revolutionary brotherhood, there is otherwise little that is similar externally. But in one respect they are absolutely *alike:* each part is distinctly broken into two almost equal halves. This can be seen with particular clarity from the second act on:

II. Scene with the tarpaulin   → mutiny
III. Mourning for Vakulinchuk → angry demonstration
IV. Lyrical fraternization   → shooting
V. Axiously awaiting the fleet → triumph

Moreover, at the "transition" point of each part, the halt has its own peculiar kind of *caesura.*

In one part (III), this is a few shots of clenched fists, through which the theme of mourning the dead leaps into the theme of fury.

In another part (IV), this is a sub-title—"*SUDDENLY*"— cutting off the scene of fraternization, and projecting it into the scene of the shooting.

The motionless muzzles of the rifles (in Part II). The gaping mouths of the guns (in Part V). And the cry of "Brothers," upsetting the awful pause of waiting, in an explosion of brotherly feeling—in both moments.

And it should be further noted that the transition within each part is not merely a transition to a merely *different* mood, to a merely *different* rhythm, to a merely *different* event, but each time the transition is to a sharply opposite quality. Not merely contrasting, but *opposite,* for each time it *images exactly that theme from the opposite point of view,* along with the theme that *inevitably grows from it.*

The explosion of mutiny after the breaking point of oppression has been reached, under the pointed rifles (Part II).

Or the explosion of wrath, organically breaking from the theme of mass mourning for the murdered (Part III).

The shooting on the steps as an organic "deduction" of the reaction to the fraternal embrace between the *Potemkin's* rebels and the people of Odessa (Part IV), and so on.

The unity of such a canon, recurring in *each act* of the drama, is already self-evident.

But when we look at the work as a whole, we shall see that such is the whole structure of *Potemkin*.

Actually, near the middle, the film as a whole is cut by the dead halt of a *caesura;* the stormy action of the beginning is completely halted in order to take a fresh start for the second half of the film. This similar *caesura,* within the film as a whole, is made by the episode of the dead Vakulinchuk and the harbor mists.

For the entire film this episode is a halt before the same sort of transfer that occurs in those moments cited above within the separate parts. And with this moment the theme, breaking the ring forged by the sides of one rebellious battleship, bursts into the embrace of a whole city which is topographically *opposed to the ship,* but is in feeling fused into a unity with it; a unity that is, however, broken away from it by the soldiers' boots descending the steps at that moment when the theme once more returns to the drama at sea.

We see how organic is the progressive development of the theme, and at the same time we also see how the structure of *Potemkin,* as a whole, flows from this movement of the theme, which operates *for the whole* exactly as it does *for its fractional members.*

Genre

The genre approach requires the critic to deal with a whole category of film types (*genre,* in fact, is the French word for *kind* or *type*). The concept of grouping literary works into different classifications dates back some 2500 years to Aristotle's fragmentary *Poetics.* In that work, Aristotle divides poetry into four major categories—epic, tragic, comic, and dithyrambic (irregular, lyrical)—and then proceeds to examine, in detail, the particular form, characteristics, and imperatives of each category. Tragedy, according to Aristotle, imitates an action that is both complete in itself and contains a clearly recognizable beginning, middle, and end. Tragedy also makes use of a dramatic rather than narrative form and sets out to fulfill a specific objective, a catharsis: by arousing feelings of pity and fear in the audience, the drama enables them to experience a powerful release of emotions. Aristotle's discussion of tragedy and other categories of poetry is, of course, far more complex and extensive than this summary indicates, but for our purposes here the important thing to note is that his method of classification was both analytic and systematic.

Though Aristotle was simply describing the literature of his day, his observations were presented with such authority that succeeding generations of poets and playwrights began to elevate *Poetics* to the status of dogma. Thus, by the eighteenth century neoclassic critics were arguing that a literary work could not be considered a "true" tragedy unless it conformed to all the criteria set forth by Aristotle. Plays such as *Hamlet* and *Macbeth*, for example, were not tragedies in the classical sense because both included scenes that were essentially comic in nature: the gravediggers in *Hamlet* and the drunken porter in *Macbeth*. Shakespeare, by mixing comedy with tragedy, had violated the classical notion of the separateness of each genre. This prescriptive attitude, which regulated dramatic conventions in England and France for over 100 years, was known as classical genre theory.

By contrast, the modern school of genre theory makes no attempt to establish fixed rules. Rather, it simply sets out to describe, as carefully as possible, the purpose (or imperative), form, and conventions of a type. Furthermore, modern genre studies do not exclusively restrict themselves to narrow areas of concern such as the work's subject, technique, or country of origin. In some film criticism references may be made to "the French film," "the Russian film," "the Japanese film," and so on, but obviously nothing exists that is remotely similar to what these terms imply: a homogenous, national style of film making. By the same token, even though a group of films may employ the same technique—say, animation—this does not elevate all animated films to genre status; a world of differences, for example, separates Walt Disney's *Bambi* (1943) from Halas and Batchelor's *Animal Farm* (1955). Nor can it be assumed that films which deal with the same subject automatically constitute a genre. War films, for example, share no common purpose. Some glorify war as a noble venture, some portray it as an unfortunate but necessary adjunct to human history, and some condemn it as a shameful and unnecessary waste of human life and resources. On the other hand, a species such as the horror film *does* constitute a true genre, because all horror films share the same purpose, form, and stock of devices or conventions.

The purpose of the horror film can be stated easily enough: to frighten the audience. And in terms of form and structure, the narratives tend to unfold in certain characteristic patterns. One typical formula is to have some monstrous and/or deformed creature unleashed on society, often through the meddling of man or an accident of nature. There follows a series of inexplicable incidents or deaths, usually viewed through the eyes of the ingenue, hero, or both; then comes the confirmation of what previously they had only suspected; and finally, after the protagonists have experienced a number of narrow escapes, the destruction of the creature (or creatures) is successfully accomplished. In addition, all horror films utilize a vast range of conventions and devices: ruined castles, crumbling manors, blasted heaths, thick fog, sliding panels, dark and secret passageways, dimly lit rooms, intricate chemical apparatus, strange and mysterious deaths. The possibilities are seemingly unlimited.

The starting point for a genre study is to determine whether or not the group of films under consideration does indeed constitute a true genre. As indicated above, the writer should examine three factors in making this decision: purpose, form, and conventions.

In defining the purpose of a given genre, the writer must be as *specific* as possible. In other words, if he cannot come up with a distinct and precise objective which all these films have in common, he cannot consider them a genre. The purpose of the horror films, as noted, is simply to frighten the audience. Arthur Knight, in an essay on Italian neorealist films (see pp. 183–193), suggests that this particular genre sets out to "show things as they are." The purpose of a genre may be moral, aesthetic, or even (as with horror films) purely frivolous; but it must be relatively specific.

If the films do seem to possess a common purpose, several other factors should be considered: similarities in narrative pattern, characteristic conventions or devices, and uniformity of visual and/or aural qualities.

For instance, the narrative pattern of the psychological thriller, of which Hitchcock's films are outstanding examples, is fairly characteristic. Typically, a rather ordinary person finds himself, by some quirk of fate, thrown into difficult and exceptional circumstances; though he doesn't understand the precise identity or

source of this threat, he must cope with it as best he can. Hitchcock employed this same pattern in *Rear Window* (1954), *North
by Northwest* (1959), *Psycho* (1960), and *Marnie.*

In addition most genres share similar conventions, devices, or
"pieces of business." Most of Hitchcock's films employ what he
calls a "MacGuffin"; the MacGuffin is a pretext for the plot, the
papers or plans the spies are after. To the characters, the Mac-
Guffin must seem vitally important, but for the director it is
merely a means for establishing conflict and getting the story
under way. Science fiction films, of course, rely heavily on devices:
time machines, extraordinary space vehicles, and elaborate scientific equipment for sending and receiving communications with
other planets. The James Bond films and the host of imitators
that followed (*Our Man Flint* [1966] and the Matt Helm movies
with Dean Martin) also show a predilection for spy gadgetry.
Some genres spawn their own conventions. Many of those in the
average western, for example, haven't changed substantially since
Edwin S. Porter made the "Great Train Robbery": the fight on
the moving train, the laughable dude from the East, the chase
and the shoot-out.

The films of some genres exhibit markedly uniform visual and
aural characteristics. Cinéma vérité (literally "direct cinema")
sets out to capture reality as spontaneously and truthfully as
possible. Hand-held cameras and fast film stock are nearly always
the norm; therefore, most cinéma vérité films look similar with
their grainy image characteristics, sudden and jerky camera
movements, mostly eye-level and apparently uncomposed shots.
Likewise, extensive use of computer graphics by film makers such
as Jordan Belson, John Whitney, and his sons John Jr., Michael,
and Mark give their films similar visual qualities.

Genre studies can make a very solid contribution to the body
of film criticism, as they focus attention not only on the similarities between certain types of films, but also on the various stages
of development that a particular genre has undergone. For example, a genre study might show how a complex film narrative like
Peckinpah's *The Wild Bunch* evolved from simpler, more primitive films such as Porter's "The Great Train Robbery"; or how
the early film fantasies of Georges Méliès (especially "A Trip to
the Moon" [1902], "The Impossible Voyage" [1904], and "The

Conquest of the Pole" [1912]) with their emphasis on the extraordinary served as precursors to the modern science fiction film.

If there is any drawback to genre studies, it is the tendency to slight, perhaps even ignore, the unique qualities of individual films because of the emphasis on shared characteristics. For instance, John Ford's *Stagecoach* (1939) represents a marvelous example of the western: there are impressive panoramic shots of Monument Valley, Utah, a breathtaking chase sequence, an unspoken moral code that binds the misfits together, and so forth. However, to simply categorize those features of *Stagecoach* that are characteristic of the type while ignoring its unique artistic qualities, such as the carefully composed shots, the rhythms, and the well-balanced organization, would be to render a great disservice to the film. Furthermore, genre types begin to "break down" when the overzealous critic attempts to force a particular film or group of films into an inappropriate category. Alfred Hitchcock's *Psycho*, for example, employs a number of features that are, for Hitchcock, uncharacteristic: extensive use of terror, the Gothic-style mansion on the hill, and the absence of a sympathetic viewpoint character. With the exception of the last item, however, the other features are extremely characteristic of the horror film. But certainly it would be a mistake to categorize *Psycho* as a horror film, for it is utterly devoid of the basic elements of all true horror films: "black magic" and/or supernaturalism.

The following essay, Arthur Knight's "The Course of Italian Neo-Realism," employs a genre approach in order to describe a particular type of film that came into being shortly after World War II. Notice how Knight first describes the historical context surrounding the rise of the neorealist film, then goes on to identify the genre's aesthetic intentions, its characteristic features, and its stock of conventions.

THE COURSE OF ITALIAN NEO-REALISM
Arthur Knight

There had been signs of a new vitality in the Italian studios at the very end of the silent era, evidence that the film makers were beginning to catch up with the technical mastery that existed elsewhere. Under the leadership of Alessandro Blasetti, both as a director and as editor of the magazine *Cinematografo*, Italian films were breaking out of their moribund tradition of old-fashioned spectacles and cliché *romanzas*. Blasetti's first film *Sole* (1929) was a drama based on Mussolini's vast project of draining the Pontine marshes. Its immediate success suggested the possibility of turning to other positive aspects of the contemporary scene as sources for filmic material. But the established producers were hesitant; and as they waited, sound arrived to put an end for the moment to Blasetti's dream. The studios turned promptly to the stage for both themes and actors, and the sweet strains of Neapolitan love songs effectively drowned out any plea for greater realism or more imaginative techniques. The early years of sound in Italy were dominated by the musicals, and by romances and boudoir farces drawn from stage plays—"white telephone films," the Italians called them because so much of the action seemed to center about the white telephone in the heroine's bedchamber.

As noted earlier, the Fascist government at first took little interest in the motion-picture field. There was, of course, official encouragement for historical films celebrating the rise of the Fascist party or re-creating the life and times of such popular heroes as Garibaldi, Ettore Fieramosca and Salvator Rosa, but nothing more tangible. Fascist interests were, at that time, satisfactorily served by the flow of propaganda shorts and newsreels turned out by the government-owned LUCE. When the talkies arrived in 1930 this company promptly added three sound trucks to its equipment, with the result that impassioned harangues by Mussolini became part of all their newsreels. These, together with any other shorts turned out by LUCE, were shown by government decree in every motion-picture house throughout Italy. But aside from such minor inconveniences, Italian producers, distributors and exhibitors were left pretty much to their own devices until 1935. Between 1935 and 1940, however, things began to change. Mussolini was launching those wars and campaigns through which he hoped to extend the Italian empire and increase his own stature. National feeling, national pride had to be whipped up to a fever pitch. It was during this period that the government gradually gained control of the motion-picture industry, achieving this not by outright ownership but by a weird and complicated form of patronage that the State held out to the eighteen accredited producing studios. Producers now could easily borrow up to 60 per cent of the cost of a picture from the State-controlled banks; if they were able to show that their film was either popular, artistic, or propagandistically useful, they had only to repay a small portion of the loan. Under such conditions, it became virtually impossible for a studio to lose money no matter how unsuccessful its pictures might be. Before long the studios were offering top jobs to political favorites because of their ability to wangle even more profitable concessions from the venal officials directing the banks and the State credit agencies. When Mussolini's son Vittorio entered the industry as head of Europa Films, Italy's largest studio, the pattern of nepotism and patronage was complete.

The government further increased its influence over the industry when it decreed that all foreign films shown in Italy had to be dubbed, and that the dubbing had to be done by Italians. This not only created more film jobs, it also made it simple to eliminate from foreign imports any sentiments that were not fully in accord with Fascist ideology—a neat, unobtrusive form of censorship. At the same time, the State awarded the valuable licenses for dubbing and distributing these films to those studios that produced the most or the most expensive pictures each year— a form of patronage that proved completely demoralizing. Indeed, no system could have been more ideally designed to encourage wastefulness and to discourage creativity.

Considering the amount of control the government actually held over the film industry both economically and by the appointment of political favorites to key positions, it is surprising how few of the pictures were made as outright Fascist propaganda. The Italians were satisfied, it would seem, with a primarily negative propaganda. They were content if their film simply ignored all ideas of democracy, civil rights, civil liberties or similarly "decadent" notions. Ettore Margadonna, one of the leading historians of the Italian film, has estimated that "out of more than five hundred feature films [produced between 1930 and 1942], those which were one hundred per cent Fascist in content may be counted on the fingers of one hand." These exceptions would include *Black Shirt* (1933), Blasetti's *Old Guard* (1935), *The Siege of the Alcázar* (1940), proudly revealing Italy's part in the Spanish Civil War, and Carmine Gallone's soporific extravaganza *Scipio Africanus* (1937). Rumored to have been written by Benito Mussolini himself, it presumed to see in the ancient Italian victory in Africa the heroic counterpart of Mussolini's own campaign in Ethiopia. Filmed in Africa and on the giant stages of the new, State-financed Cinecittà, it was one of the most costly, most opulent productions of all time—and also one of the most overblown. Critics delighted in pointing to the telephone poles that sprouted from the hilltops of Imperial Rome, the wrist watches on the Roman legionnaires, and to the stupefying emptiness of the vast spectacle. Nevertheless, because it was an official film, the government made special efforts to have it shown abroad. Its reception did little to enhance the reputation of the Italian film makers. A few of the Italian opera films were also exported, notably Gallone's *The Dream of Butterfly* (1939), featuring long passages from Puccini's opera beautifully performed by Maria Cebotari, and a tear-stained story of a diva who, like Butterfly herself, loved not wisely but well. Aside from these— nothing.

But if the corrupt and corrupting Italian studios were unable to produce a masterpiece, at least they enabled talented people to gain a mastery of their art. Clearly, the neo-realist movement that burst forth with such vitality after the war could only have come from men whose artistic impulses had long been bottled up, from men who knew the techniques of film making but lacked the opportunity to use them significantly. Many had been trained at the government-operated Centro Sperimentale, the official film school in Rome. Many had worked under the dispiriting studio conditions that marked the final years of Fascism. Vittorio De Sica, for example, had alternated between stage and screen as a matinee idol throughout the thirties. He turned to directing in 1940, specializing in sentimental comedies which he handled with a good deal of superficial charm and, on occasion, sharp insights into the behavior of children. Roberto Rossellini worked on a number of documentaries before being assigned as assistant director on *The White Ship* (1941), a wartime propaganda film almost totally lacking in human feeling. Two more features, *The Return of the Pilot* (1942) and *The Man of the Cross* (1943), seem to have been equally devoid of any hint of his postwar style. Of the old guard, only Alessandro Blasetti gave any suggestion of the new themes and new techniques that lay ahead. His *Four Steps in the Clouds* (1943) for a moment took the Italian film out of the world of "white telephones" and official attitudes. It was a touching, warm-hearted comedy in which a kindly man from the city finds himself pretending to be the husband of a country girl he has met by chance—and the father of her unborn child. Though far from political, its picture of peasant life, its Italian peasant types and natural settings strongly foreshadowed the neo-realist films of the postwar era. Indeed, when *Four Steps* was first shown in New York, undated, critics assumed it had been made *after* the war, as part of the movement touched off by *Open City*.

For all its excellences, *Four Steps in the Clouds* remains a modest work, a harbinger. But late in 1942, when Mussolini's hold on his people was fast disintegrating, there appeared Luchino Visconti's *Ossessione*, a true masterpiece that contained all the seeds of the postwar neo-realist movement—the concern for people, the use of natural settings and types, the overwhelming sense of looking at life as it really is. An adaptation (although uncredited) of James M. Cain's *The Postman Always Rings Twice*, its sordid theme was played against the background of a small *trattoria* on the marshes of the Po and a fair at Ancona. And though Visconti used such familiar Italian actors as Massimo Girotti, Clara Calamai and Elio Marcuzzo, under his direction they performed with a naturalism that blended with the sweaty peasants who crowded the bar at the shabby inn and thronged the amusement booths of the *festa*. The camera work was always arresting, using long traveling shots to keep the principals in screen center as they moved through the crowds, using concealed cameras for sequences in public parks and streets, mounting the camera on a crane to rise from a close-up of an actor to panoramas of an entire landscape within a single shot. Here were the faces of real Italians, the sights and sounds of everyday Italy mobilized upon the screen to tell a powerful and affecting story. It was a revelation, a film so far beyond anything produced in the twenty years of Fascism that its impression upon other Italian film makers could only have been profound. Unfortunately, it is a revelation that few Americans seem destined to share. Not only was Visconti's film a fairly flagrant violation of copyright, but the film rights to Cain's novel already belonged to M-G-M, which produced its own version of the story in 1946. M-G-M has been adamant in refusing to permit prints of *Ossessione* to enter the United States.

As the war progressed, film making in Italy became increasingly chaotic (as did life itself). Loyalties were divided. Some favored the Allies—or thought the Axis a losing cause; some clung to their Fascist beliefs. After the fall of Mussolini, with war still ravaging the south and the Nazis occupying the remainder of the peninsula, film making came to a virtual standstill. In 1944 only sixteen pictures were produced in Italy, most of them coming from Scalera's studio in Venice, the last stronghold of the Fascist

elements in the industry. Meanwhile, anti-fascists went into
hiding, awaiting the liberation of the Allied forces, awaiting the
withdrawal of the Nazi army of occupation. Late in 1944, even
before the Germans had completed their evacuation of Rome,
Roberto Rossellini was already at work on *Open City*, the key
film in the entire neo-realist Italian revival. In it he sought to
re-create, as accurately as possible, the tensions, the trials and
the heroic resistance of the common people of Rome during the
years of the Nazi occupation. Aside from the principals, few in
the cast were professional actors. Many, indeed, were simply
citizens—or Nazi soldiers—photographed on the fly by cameras
concealed on rooftops or hidden in cars. Little of the film was
shot in a studio, partly for financial reasons, partly because Rossellini (and Cesare Zavattini, who wrote the script) sensed that
the documentary value of actual streets, apartments and court-
yards would heighten the authenticity of their story.

What emerged was a film strikingly unlike anything that had
been seen before. Technically, it was far from flawless. Rossellini
had been forced to use whatever scraps of film stock he could lay
his hands on, while the lighting—particularly in those interiors
not taken in a studio—was often too weak for dramatic effects or
even adequate modeling. Indeed, shooting had to be abandoned
entirely several times while the director set about raising the
necessary funds to continue. But the very passion that had inspired the production of *Open City* seemed to create the centrif-
ugal force that held it all together. Its roughness, its lack of finish
became a virtue. And the cumulative power of Rossellini's feeling
for his subject was translated into a visual intensity that made the
picture sometimes almost unbearable to watch. Here was true
realism—the raw life of a tragic era. "This is the way things are,"
said Rossellini in presenting his film. It became the credo of the
entire neo-realist movement.

Within the next five years there appeared in Italy a cycle of
films in every way as remarkable and exciting as the great Russian
pictures of the late twenties—and inspired, like them, by the
sudden discovery of a national identity and the simultaneous
liberation of creative talents. The complete breakdown of the
Fascist régime removed all previous restraints. The years of repres-
sion under the Nazi occupation forces, the disenchantment under
the Allies produced a social awareness that found its fullest
expression in the neo-realist movement. At the outset, the mere
ability to treat dispassionately the daily life of the ordinary Italian
was inspiration enough for directors like Rossellini and De Sica.
Rossellini's *Paisan* (1946) was an epic study of the last months

of war in Italy. De Sica, the former matinee idol, revealed again his concern for children in *Shoeshine* (1946), but with a depth and passion unsuspected from his earlier films. It is a poignant, muted tale of an appealing group of Roman street urchins caught up in the black market that swept through Italy during the war years. The boys are jailed, then friend is set against friend so that their captors may gain a little more information on the gangsters who have been using them. De Sica makes it amply clear that the authorities are neither brutal nor stupid, merely hard pressed. But because they take the easy, obvious course, friends become enemies and murder is the final outcome. All of this is offered without either bitterness or cynicism as a dramatization of actual conditions. And if his revelations disturbed his audience it was, after all, up to them as citizens to do something about it. In such films can be detected the emergence of a truly democratic spirit—the objective presentation of social fact, with social action left to the conscience and the intelligence of the viewer.

With Rossellini and De Sica as its leaders, the neo-realist movement quickly gathered momentum and was confirmed in the work of a dozen or more directors in the period immediately after the war. Drawn irresistibly to social themes, they were united by a common philosophy that was perhaps most clearly expressed in Luigi Zampa's *To Live in Peace* (1946). Zampa selected an incident from the very end of the war to suggest that all men—even Nazis—could live together in friendship if they followed their instincts instead of their ideologies. An Italian farmer has given shelter to two American soldiers caught behind the German lines, one white and one colored. During the night the German sentry from the village comes to the farm. In order to cover up the noises of the Negro drinking in the cellar, the farmer gets the German drunk. Suddenly the American bursts out of his hiding place, and there is a suspenseful moment as Nazi and Negro face each other. But all hate, all conflicting ideology has been drowned in the wine. The two wrap their arms around each other and go roaring through the village, "The war is over—Der krieg ist kaput." In *Angelina* (1947), Zampa reiterated the same theme, that man's better instincts are subverted by his blind obedience to orders. In the title role, Anna Magnani gave a wonderfully funny and sympathetic performance as a working-class housewife who becomes the leader of all the women in her neighborhood against the local politicians and landlords.

Other directors took actual incidents from the postwar scene to create images of shocking or pitiable truth. In the first half of

Tragic Hunt (1947), Giuseppe De Santis drew a remarkable picture of the chaos, the lawlessness that followed the end of hostilities in northern Italy, and although a taste for melodrama marred its second part, his scenes of peasants organizing and fighting for the right to return to their land were both moving and convincing. Also quite melodramatic (almost inevitably) was Alberto Lattuada's *Without Pity* (1947), centered on another serious postwar problem in Italy, the Negro G.I.'s who had deserted the Army and were living lawlessly in the Tombolo, north of Leghorn. There was sensitivity in this story of a Negro and his love for a white prostitute, but sensationalism as well. (The film was cut drastically for exhibition in the United States.) From Visconti, the director of *Ossessione,* came a ponderous but searching and indubitably sincere study of the lives of impoverished Sicilian fishermen, *The Earth Trembles* (1948), made documentary-fashion without actors or studio settings—and in a dialect so special that not even all Italians could follow it. Again it was a film that said, with sympathy: "This is the way things are. What are we going to do about it?"

Out of all these films—and many more—there emerged the image of the ordinary Italian. With a vividness and humanity unequaled by any other nation, the drama of commonplace joys and sorrows was projected from the screen. Curiously enough, such pictures were not at first too well received in Italy itself. Perhaps they reflected the ordinary too accurately. What the Italians wanted was the glitter, the glamour, the romance of the Hollywood movies after their years of misery and privation. In any case, it was the critical reception abroad of such pictures as *Open City, Shoeshine, Bicycle Thief* and *To Live in Peace* that opened the eyes of most Italians to what they really had. All of them proved far more successful on their subsequent runs in their native land than when first released.

As economic stability began to return to Italy, the Italian producers began to consolidate their gains. In Cinecittà, just outside Rome, they had not only the largest and best equipped studios in all Europe but also, at the film school there, a well-trained corps of artists and technicians to draw upon. Furthermore, the new government took a healthy interest in film production, recognizing its value as a source both of good-will and of revenue for the country. Outstanding pictures were rewarded with special tax rebates. As an additional aid to the home industry, acting on a plan put forward by the Italian producers themselves, the government permitted the American studios to

take out of the country a portion of their war-frozen dollars provided that some of this money were allocated to the development
of a market in the United States for Italian pictures. In 1950 the
American producers agreed—and found themselves in the unprecedented position of actively encouraging the growth of a
rival industry in their own country. Except for the British, no
nation has ever before made such a concerted effort to break into
the American market. To overcome the resistance of the average
moviegoer to subtitled foreign films, they even set up their own
dubbing studios in New York, matching the voices of Broadway
actors to the lips of the Italian performers. The experiment failed.
The contrast between Italian gesture and stage English all but
destroyed the illusion of reality the directors sought to achieve;
the pictures were neither good enough for the art-house circuits
nor popular enough for the neighborhood chains. A few of the
more spectacular exploitation items, like *Attila* (1958), were
bought and adapted by American firms. Others—*Ulysses* (1955),
War and Peace (1957), *Tempest* (1959)—have been costly co-
productions with American firms, forcing the American box office
with Hollywood's stars and budgets, and the Italian flair for
elaborate pageantry.

Indeed, the Italians have become so terribly anxious for wide
box-office approval that, within the past few years, the original
tenets of neo-realism have been increasingly distorted. *Bitter Rice*
(1949), for example, begins as a tale of migratory rice workers
in northern Italy, but soon degenerates into a sordid melodrama
of rape and violence. Both *Rome, 11 o'Clock* (1952) and *Three
Forbidden Stories* (1953) tastelessly exploit an actual tragedy that
shocked all Italy. Over two hundred girls had turned up at an
office in response to an ad for a single position, thronging the
stairs to await their turn. When the stairs gave way, scores were
killed or injured. In *Rome, 11 o'Clock*, this incident is re-created
and then, flash-back fashion, the film goes into the lives of several
of the victims—a girl who had left home to live with an artist, a
prostitute who wants to go straight, a girl disillusioned about
finding a glamour job in radio, a shy girl in search of her first
position. In *Three Forbidden Stories* the treatment is even more
frankly sensational. One of its heroines is a lesbian, another a
dope addict.

Most of the recent "realistic" films from Italy have had their
origin in similar incidents, in real-life stories gleaned from the
newspapers. All too often, however, the stories built out from
these backgrounds have been an exploitation rather than a

revelation of their themes. True, reality has not been prettied up in these films, as is so often the case with our own American pictures. On the contrary, there seems to be a concentrated effort to make everything as grim as possible—"this is the way things are"—but with increasing emphasis on such marketable aspects of reality as sex and sadism. And in place of the earthy, hearty Anna Magnani, the Italian screen abounded with cover girls like Gina Lollobrigida, Silvana Magano, Silvana Pampanini, Sophia Loren and Eleanora Rossi-Drago—sleek, well-developed creatures, delightful to look at, but scarcely ideal as the heroines of neo-realistic dramas. In fact, as so often happens, the word itself has become little more than a catch-phrase today. The Italian cinema may continue to advertise its neo-realism, but what we have been seeing of late is largely a series of melodramatic shockers photographed against natural exteriors.

In the meantime, several neo-neorealisms have emerged that hold new promise for the Italian screen—if ever the producers find the courage to follow them up. All of them are based firmly in the everyday life of ordinary Italians and motivated by a sympathy and affection for the common man. But a new dimension has been added, a new element of comedy, fantasy, even poetry. We can see now that De Sica's strange, fanciful *Miracle in Milan* (1951), with its hoboes soaring on broomsticks high above Milan's cathedral, was in fact the point of departure for this whole new genre. Renato Castellani's *Two Cents' Worth of Hope* (1952) and Luigi Comencini's *Bread, Love and Dreams* (1953), for example, created a fine sense of the reality of small-town life in the Italian hills, then used this as the background for broad comedy that also veered off into fantasy. Federico Fellini's *La Strada* (1954), a somber, tragic study of an itinerant sideshow strong man and a simple-minded girl clown, explored a new blending of realism and poetry, a heightening of emotion through skillfully stylized performances juxtaposed against natural backgrounds. *Love in the City* (1954), a project conceived and organized by Cesare Zavattini and directed by half a dozen youthful enthusiasts, also seems to mark a new direction. Here the emphasis is returned again to documentary realism, with people re-enacting their own tragedies or speaking urgently of their lives and problems directly in front of the cameras and microphones. But by skillful use of the camera, by dubbing and editing, Zavattini has transformed simple documentation into genuinely artistic creation.

Here is fresh ore for the Italian film, new directions to be explored and developed with all the passion and enthusiasm that marked the renaissance of the Italian film industry ten years ago. It is evident that the directors still have abundant vitality to tackle new themes and to work in new styles. The question now seems to be, will the Italian producers, obsessed with dreams of conquering the international market, permit them to do so? Will they be allowed to follow the lines sketched in by De Sica, Fellini, Castellani, Comencini, Antonioni and Zavattini? Or must they dissipate their talents on sordid studies of passionate drug addicts and frustrated telephone girls? Such pictures, sold not on their artistry but on their sensationalism, can only result in the eventual suffocation of first the art, and then the industry itself. For it is the artists in film—the directors and the writers—who tap the new and occasionally profitable veins of cinematic ore. The odd thing about movies is that once the industrial side moves in and begins to commercialize the operation, the outcome is frequently disappointing to the audiences, to the artists, and ultimately to the producers themselves.

Other Approaches

The critical approaches discussed in this chapter do not, of course, exhaust the ways in which a film or group of films can be analyzed. Film history (as distinguished from the study of film as it reflects a historical period), the relationship of film to other arts, the use of point of view in film, studies of structural and organizational problems, analysis of metaphors and symbols in films, studies of editing styles—all represent valid, defensible critical approaches.

The quality of criticism directed at any art is probably a good indication of the stage of development that the art has attained. To reiterate a point made earlier, good criticism not only calls public attention to the excellent and meritorious, but also renders the new and complex more accessible to greater numbers of people. Furthermore, criticism provides the artist with a thoughtful, objective analysis of his work. And perhaps most importantly, criticism helps to develop more astute, informed, and perceptive audiences; and when the sophistication of the audience increases, the artist's potential for creative achievement expands proportionally. Thus, in order to realize the maximum evolution of his talent, the artist is to a large degree dependent upon his audience. As Walt Whitman once wrote, "To have great poets, there must be great audiences too."

REFERENCES

1. Andrew Sarris, ed., *Interviews with Film Directors* (New York: Avon Books, 1967), p. 208.

2. Joseph Gelmis, ed., *The Film Director as Superstar* (Garden City, N.J.; Doubleday & Company, Inc., 1970), p. 77.

3. John Simon, *Private Screenings* (New York: Berkeley Medallion, 1967), p. 8.

4. David Paletz, "Judith Crist: An Interview with a Big-Time Critic," *Film Quarterly* 22 (Fall 1968): 28.

5. Ibid., p. 28.

6. Ibid., pp. 27–30.

7. Simon, pp. 14–15.

8. Pauline Kael, *I Lost It at the Movies* (New York: Bantam Books, 1966), pp. 277–78.

9. Tom Milne, ed., *Godard on Godard* (New York: Viking Press, 1972), p. 172.

10. Simon, p. 17.

11. Harry M. Geduld, ed., *Film Makers on Film Making* (Bloomington, Ind.: Indiana University Press, 1967), p. 79.

12. Jay Leyda, ed., *Sergei Eisenstein's "Film Form"* (New York: Harcourt Brace Jovanovich, 1949), p. 48.

13. Gene Youngblood, *Expanded Cinema* (New York: E. P. Dutton & Co., Inc., 1970), p. 75.

14. Sarris, pp. 208–09.

15. Ibid., p. 521.

16. Pauline Kael, *I Lost It at the Movies* (New York: Bantam Books, 1966), p. 278.

17. Pauline Kael, *The Citizen Kane Book* (Boston: Little, Brown and Company, 1971), p. 74.

18. Siegfried Kracauer, *From Caligari to Hitler* (Princeton, N.J.: Princeton University Press, 1947), p. 5.

19. Gerald Mast, *A Short History of the Movies* (New York: Bobbs-Merrill Company, Inc., 1971), pp. 280–81.

20. Edward Mapp, *Blacks in American Films: Today and Yesterday* (Metuchen, N.J.: The Scarecrow Press, Inc., 1972), pp. 30–31.

21. Dwight MacDonald, *On Movies* (New York: Berkeley Medallion, 1969), pp. 63–65.

22. Carlos Fuentes, "The Discreet Charm of Luis Buñuel," *The New York Times Magazine* (March 11, 1973): 48.

23. Ibid., p. 86.

24. Gelmis, p. 145.

25. MacDonald, p. 53.

26. C. G. Crisp, *François Truffaut* (New York: Praeger, 1972), p. 28.

27. François Truffaut, *Hitchcock* (New York: Simon and Schuster, 1967), p. 13.

28. Ibid., p. 8.

29. T. S. Eliot, *The Sacred Wood* (New York: University Paperbacks, 1920), p. 100.

30. MacDonald, p. 10.

31. Susan Sontag, *Against Interpretation* (New York: Dell Publishing Co., Inc., 1967), p. 177.

32. Kael, *I Lost It at the Movies*, p. 168.

33. Alain Robbe-Grillet, *Last Year at Marienbad* (New York: Grove Press, 1962), p. 14.

A GLOSSARY OF IMPORTANT FILM TERMS

AUDIO Synonymous with sound and usually refers to the sound portion of the film.

BLIMP A special housing which encases a camera used to record dialogue; the housing serves to soundproof the noise of the camera so it will not be picked up by the recording microphone.

CAMERA ANGLE Refers to the angle that exists between the camera and the subject; a "normal" angle corresponds to an eye-level view; "low" angle is below eye level; "high" angle, of course, would be located above eye level.

CAMERA, MOTION PICTURE Photographic instrument which makes a series of intermittent photographs on a strip of sensitized film which, when projected, produces the illusion of movement.

CAMERAMAN Individual who operates the motion picture camera, or who contributes to its operation.

CAMERA-STYLO Literally, "camera pen." An expression invented by French film maker and theorist Alexandre Astruc, who was convinced that the film maker could employ his camera to deal with "any sphere of thought," just as writers used pens to record their thoughts.

CLIP Small piece of film extracted from a larger section of film, usually to illustrate something specific such as a highly dramatic moment or an unusual technical accomplishment.

CLOSE-UP A shot taken very close to a subject; if it were taken of a man, it would only show his head and shoulders.

CUT The sudden transition from one shot to another produced by splicing separate shots of film together; with few exceptions, a cut is synonymous with a change in camera position.

and

"CUT!" The command, usually uttered by the director, to stop the recording of a shot; this order is given when the director is satisfied with the execution of the shot or scene.

CUTAWAY When the audience's attention is momentarily diverted from the main action to a subordinate action; a cutaway is usually employed as a plot device to prolong suspense.

DAILIES See **RUSHES.**

DEVELOP, DEVELOPMENT A chemical treatment of the exposed film so as to make the latent image—the visible image registered on the film when the film has been exposed to light—visible.

DIRECTOR Usually, the individual who is most responsible for the shape of the finished film; he supervises the action and the dialogue that occurs before the camera.

DISSOLVE An optical effect whereby one shot gradually disappears as another simultaneously takes its place.

DOUBLE A look-alike actor who stands in for one of the main players, usually to perform a dangerous stunt.

DOUBLE-EXPOSURE The same strip of film is exposed on two different occasions; consequently, when the film is developed, two superimposed images are visible.

DUB, DUBBING (sometimes called **lip-sync**) Matching separately recorded sound to the lip movements of the actor on the screen. Dubbing can also be used to record musical scores.

EDITING Splicing and assembling together the separate shots of the film in their proper continuity.

> **CONTINUITY EDITING** Portrays action in a "realistic" manner; the emphasis is on the creation of a continuous flow of events, apparently uninterrupted; the unities of space and time are fairly closely adhered to.

> **DYNAMIC EDITING** Fragments the action, and proceeds on the basis of juxtaposition and contrasts; the unities of time and space are frequently ignored.

EDITOR The individual responsible for assembling shots and audio in proper continuity.

ESTABLISHING SHOT A segment of film that quickly sets the scene and creates a mood.

FADE An optical effect whereby a shot gradually darkens to blackness—a **fade-out;** or lightens to reveal a new image—a **fade-in.**

FAST MOTION The film moves through the camera at a slower than normal rate of speed; when film recorded in this fashion is projected, the action appears faster than normal.

FILM A thin strip of celluloid or other transparent material with perforations along the sides that is coated with light-sensitive emulsion and is capable of producing photographic images.

FINE CUT   An editorial stage in the film's development; the fine cut, a more completed version of the film, follows the rough cut; as the film moves towards its final form, excess footage is edited out.

FLIP   See **WIPE.**

FOOTAGE   The length of a film, measured in feet.

FRAME   An individual, transparent picture on a strip of film.

FREEZE FRAME   In the laborartory, a single frame is duplicated many times over. Thus, when the film is projected, the reproduced frame appears to stand still on the screen or to "freeze."

HIGH KEY   A lighting technique that produces a brightly illuminated setting; often used in comedies and light dramas.

KEY LIGHT   When artificial lighting is used to illuminate an individual, an object or a set, the key light refers to the main source of light on the set.

LOCATION   Virtually any place, other than the studio or the stage, where the picture is being shot.

LOW KEY   A lighting technique whereby the setting is deliberately underilluminated in order to heighten dramatic action; often used in horror films.

MASK   Strip of film which contains opaque portions that serve to exclude or reduce light transmission. Most commonly, masks are used for special effects and trick photography.

MATCH-CUT   A filmic transition. The cuts from one shot to the next are "matched" either by action (e.g., when Dustin Hoffman in *The Graduate* leaps up from the pool towards a float and the film cuts to him landing on Mrs. Robinson in the hotel bed) or by subject matter (e.g., when the man-ape of Kubrick's *2001* knocks a bone into the air and the film cuts to a similarly shaped space station orbiting the moon).

MISE-EN-SCENE   A French term which refers to the theatrical aspects of staging a film—i.e., the use of setting, deployment of lighting, blocking of actors' physical movements, etc.

MIXING   A process consisting of combining several sound tracks into a single sound track.

MONTAGE   A cinematic method of representing reality that combines fragments of images and sounds from nature and then combines and juxtaposes them in such a way that they become something new; i.e., an image of an eye followed by an image of rushing water suggests tears. *Also,* montage is used to describe the impressionistic combination of brief shots that are used to supply a "time" or "mood" bridge in a film. A father searches the city for his son; the audience sees a brief shot of him talking to the policeman in the city park, another of him talking to the janitor at the school, and so on.

OPTICAL EFFECTS Dissolves, fades, wipes—in other words, any technique that utilizes the optical printer, which is a special mechanism that enables images from one film to be photographed onto another film by means of a special lens.

OUT OF SYNC The actor's lip movements are not in synchronization with the sound.

PAN Description of a camera movement; a pan is said to occur when the camera is held in a fixed position and rotated on a horizontal or vertical axis.

PRODUCER Individual who is responsible for the entire production of the film.

PROPS All the movable fixtures, furnishings, materials and physical properties necessary for the setting.

RAW STOCK Unexposed or unprocessed film.

REEL(S) The metal spools onto which the film is wound.

RETAKE To redo a scene in which something has gone wrong—i.e., an actor muffing a line, a technician wandering on the set.

ROUGH CUT An early editing stage in the film's development, usually the first time that the editor assembles the film from the selected takes.

RUSHES Sometimes called "Dailies." Prints developed immediately after the day's takes for the director's perusal.

SCENE Usually a series of shots that are unified by time and space; in writing, a scene would be roughly analogous to a paragraph.

SCRIPT The written blueprint for the film's production; in its initial form, the script is known as a **treatment**—a pre-production synopsis of the film; later it evolves into the **shooting script,** the final form of the script, which contains detailed and exact production instructions.

SEQUENCE A division of the film, roughly analogous to a chapter in a novel; usually a series of events that are related by time, space, or both.

SET   An artificial construction, including props, that is usually located in the studio, and simulates a locale—i.e., the main street of a small town.

SHOOTING SCRIPT   After the treatment has undergone further discussion and elaboration, the shooting script is prepared. The shooting script breaks the story down into small filmic units (i.e., shots, or scenes) and serves as a guide when the film is actually shot.

SHOT   A segment of film that appears, to the viewer, to represent a single uninterrupted running of the camera (though a single shot may, of course, actually be composed of several bits of film taken at different times).

SLOW MOTION   The film moves through the camera at a faster than normal rate of speed; when the film is projected the action takes place at a slower than normal rate of speed.

SOFT FOCUS   To film a subject slightly out of focus so that the image attains a kind of hazy quality; this technique is often used to make aging actors and actresses appear younger.

SOUND EFFECTS   Sounds which are added to the sound track in addition to the synchronized sounds of voices and music; most often sound effects represent off-camera noises.

SOUND TRACK   Either the thin band at the edge of the film that carries the sound, or a reference to the tape or optical sound track recorded separately from the visuals during the production.

SPLICE   To join end to end two separate strips of film so they make one continuous ribbon of film.

SPLIT-SCREEN, SPLIT-SCREEN MONTAGE   Two or more shots on the screen at the same time; if three different people were talking on the telephone from three different locations, the screen might be divided into three separate areas to enable the audience to view all three characters at once.

STORY BOARD   Sometimes an artist sketches out the intended camera set-ups before the actual shooting begins. These rough visuals enable the cameraman and director to preplan their set-ups.

"SUPER," SUPERIMPOSE   A type of dissolve in which both images retain the same amount of light intensity.

SYNC, SYNCHRONIZATION   Term used to describe the proper coordination of sound and image.

SYNOPSIS A bare outline of a story intended to be developed into a screenplay; the synopsis seldom runs over three paragraphs in length.

TAKE Each piece of action filmed before the camera, or to be filmed; for identification purposes, each piece of action is numbered by means of photographing a slate board which contains the necessary information.

TELEPHOTO LENS Long optical camera lens which enables the cameraman to make close shots of action taking place at a considerable distance from the camera; this lens functions similarly to a telescope.

THREE SHOT Entire image area is filled with a close shot of three people.

TILT Description of a camera movement; a tilt is said to occur when the camera is moved up and down, either obliquely or vertically.

TITLE Any written material which appears on the screen.

TREATMENT Second stage of the development of a screenplay. Further elaboration of the synopsis after the synopsis has been discussed by the director, producer, and any additional writers.

TWO SHOT Entire image area is filled with a close shot of two people.

VOICE OVER Any commentary or narration spoken over a scene by an off-camera individual.

WIDE-ANGLE LENS A short-focus camera lens which gives a wider than normal field of view to an image.

WILD SOUND Sound recorded separately from the filming. Often special sound effects are added later to the film's sound track.

WIPE Optical effect. One shot changes to another by means of a moving line that travels from side to side, or top to bottom, etc.; as the line moves across the image it "pushes off" the original image and simultaneously reveals the new image. The **flip,** another optical effect, is very similar to the wipe except that in this instance the original image appears to "turn over" revealing another image on its reverse side.

ZOOM, ZOOMING Accomplished with a special lens of variable and adjustable magnification called a zoom lens; this lens enables the cameraman to move from a wide-angle shot to a close shot and vice versa without changing the position of the camera.

SELECTED BIBLIOGRAPHY

- *General Reference Works*

Abramson, Abraham (project manager). *The New York Times Film Reviews*. 7 vols. New York: Arno Press, 1970.

Cowie, Peter. *International Film Guide*. New York: A. S. Barnes. Published annually.

————. *Seventy Years of Cinema*. New York: A. S. Barnes, 1969.

Gottesman, Ronald, and Geduld, Harry M. *Guidebook to Film*. New York: Holt, Rinehart and Winston, Inc., 1972.

Halliwell, Leslie. *The Filmgoer's Companion, Third Edition*. New York: Hill and Wang, 1970.

Michael, Paul, ed. *The American Movies Reference Book: The Sound Era*. Englewood Cliffs, N.J.: Prentice-Hall, Inc., 1970.

Manvell, Roger, ed. *The International Encyclopedia of Film*. New York: Crown Publishers, 1972.

Munden, Kenneth W., ed. *The American Film Institute Catalog, Feature Films, 1921–1930*. 2 vols. New York: R. R. Bowker Company, 1971.

Quigley, Martin, Jr., and Gertner, Richard. *Films in America, 1929–1969*. New York: Golden Press, 1970.

Pickard, R. A. E. *Dictionary of 1000 Best Films*. New York: Association Press. 1971.

Rotha, Paul, with Griffith, Richard. *The Film Till Now*. Feltham: Hamlyn Publishing Group, Ltd., 1930.

Sadoul, Georges. *Dictionary of Films*. Berkeley: University of California Press, 1965.

————. *Dictionary of Film Makers*. Berkeley: University of California Press, 1965.

Sarris, Andrew. *The American Cinema*. New York: E. P. Dutton, 1968.

- *Introductory Works on the Film Art*

Bobker, Lee R. *Elements of Film*. New York: Harcourt Brace Jovanovich, 1969.

Gessner, Robert. *The Moving Image: A Guide to Cinematic Literacy*. New York: E. P. Dutton, 1968.

Giannetti, Louis D. *Understanding Movies.* Englewood Cliffs, N.J.: Prentice-Hall, 1972.

Huss, Roy, and Silverstein, Norman. *The Film Experience.* New York: Dell Publishing Co., Inc., 1968.

Jacobs, Lewis, ed. *Introduction to the Art of the Movies.* New York: Noonday Press, 1960.

Lawson, John Howard. *Film: The Creative Process.* New York: Hill and Wang, 1967.

Lindgren, Ernest. *The Art of the Film.* New York: Macmillan, 1963.

Solomon, Stanley J. *The Film Idea.* New York: Harcourt Brace Jovanovich, 1972.

Spottiswoode, Raymond. *Film and Its Techniques.* Berkeley: University of California Press, 1951.

Stephenson, Ralph, and Debrix, J. R. *The Cinema as Art.* Baltimore: Penguin Books, 1969.

- *Film History*

Anderson, Joseph L., and Richie, Donald. *The Japanese Film: Art and Industry.* Rutland, Vermont: E. Tuttle Company, 1959.

Brownlow, Kevin. *The Parade's Gone By.* . . . New York: Alfred A. Knopf, Inc., 1968.

Ceram, C. W. *Archaeology of the Cinema.* London: Thames and Hudson, 1965.

Everson, William K. *A Pictorial History of the Western Film.* New York: Citadel Press, 1969.

Fielding, Raymond. *The American Newsreel 1911–1967.* Norman, Okla.: University of Oklahoma Press, 1972.

Fulton, Albert R. *Motion Pictures.* Norman, Okla.: University of Oklahoma Press, 1960.

Jacobs, Lewis. *The Rise of the American Film.* New York: Teachers College Press of Columbia University, 1939.

Higham, Charles, and Greenberg, Joel. *Hollywood in the Forties.* New York: Paperback Library, 1970.

Knight, Arthur. *The Liveliest Art.* New York: New American Library, 1957.

Kracauer, Siegfried. *From Caligari to Hitler.* Princeton, N.J.: Princeton University Press, 1947.

Leyda, Jay. *Kino: A History of the Russian and Soviet Film.* New York: Collier Books, 1960.

MacGowan, Kenneth. *Behind the Screen.* New York: Dell Publishing Co., 1965.

Manvell, Roger, and Fraenkel, Heinrich. *The German Cinema.* New York: Praeger, 1971.

Mast, Gerald. *A Short History of the Movies.* New York: Pegasus, 1971.

McClure, Arthur F. *The Movies: An American Idiom.* Rutherford: Fairleigh Dickinson University Press, 1971.

Ramsaye, Terry. *A Million and One Nights.* New York: Simon and Schuster, 1964.

Tyler, Parker. *Underground Film: A Critical History.* New York: Grove Press, 1969.

• *Film Theory*

Arnheim, Rudolph. *Film as Art.* Berkeley: University of California Press, 1957.

Balázs, Béla. *Theory of the Film.* New York: Dover Publications, 1970.

Bazin, André. *What is Cinema?* 2 vols. Berkeley: University of California Press, 1967 and 1971.

Eisenstein, Sergei. *Film Form.* New York: Harcourt Brace Jovanovich, 1949.

——. *The Film Sense.* New York: Harcourt Brace Jovanovich, 1949.

Kracauer, Siegfried. *Theory of Film.* London: Oxford University Press, 1960.

Linden, George W. *Reflections on the Screen.* Belmont, Calif: Wadsworth Publishing Co., 1970.

MacCann, Richard Dyer, ed. *A Montage of Theories.* New York: E. P. Dutton, 1966.

Pudovkin, V. I. *Film Technique and Film Acting.* New York: Grove Press, 1929.

Wollen, Peter. *Signs and Meaning in the Cinema.* Bloomington, Ind.: Indiana University Press, 1969.

Youngblood, Gene. *Expanded Cinema.* New York: E. P. Dutton, 1970.

- *Film Criticism*

Adler, Renata. *A Year in the Dark: Journal of a Film Critic, 1968–1969.* New York: Random House, 1969.

Agee, James. *Agee on Film: Reviews and Comments.* Boston: Beacon Press, 1964.

Bellone, Julius, ed. *Renaissance of the Film.* New York: Macmillan, 1970.

Crist, Judith. *The Private Eye, the Cowboy, and the Very Naked Girl.* New York: Paperback Library, 1970.

Kael, Pauline. *Deeper into Movies.* Boston: Little, Brown and Company, 1973.

———. *I Lost It at the Movies.* New York: Bantam, 1965.

———. *Kiss Kiss Bang Bang.* New York: Bantam, 1965.

Kauffmann, Stanley, with Henstell, Bruce. *American Film Criticism: From the Beginnings to Citizen Kane.* New York: Liveright, 1972.

———. *Figures of Light.* New York: Harper & Row, 1967.

———. *A World on Film.* New York: Dell Publishing Co., 1966.

MacDonald, Dwight. *On Movies.* New York: Berkly Publishing Corp., 1969.

Pechter, William S. *Twenty-Four Times a Second.* New York: Harper & Row, 1960.

Rhode, Eric. *Tower of Babel: Speculations on the Cinema.* Philadelphia: Chilton, 1966.

Robinson, W. R., ed. *Man and the Movies.* Baton Rouge, La.: State University Press, 1967.

Sarris, Andrew. *Confessions of a Cultist: On the Cinema, 1955/1969.* New York: Simon and Schuster, 1970.

Schickel, Richard. *Second Sight: Notes on Some Movies 1965–1970.* New York: Simon and Schuster, 1972.

Simon, John. *Movies into Film: Film Criticism 1967–1970.* New York: Dial Press, 1971.

———. *Private Screenings.* New York: Macmillan, 1967.

Sontag, Susan. *Against Interpretation and Other Essays.* New York: Dell Publishing Co., 1966.

Taylor, John Russell. *Cinema Eye, Cinema Ear.* New York: Hill and Wang, 1964.

Tyler, Parker. *The Hollywood Hallucination.* New York: Simon and Schuster, 1944.

——. *Magic and Myth of the Movies.* New York: Simon and Schuster, 1947.

——. *Screening the Sexes: Homosexuality in the Movies.* New York: Holt, Rinehart and Winston, 1972.

——. *Sex, Psyche Etcetera.* New York: Horizons Press, 1969.

Warshow, Robert. *The Immediate Experience.* Garden City, N.Y.: Doubleday–Anchor, 1964.

• *Works on Individual Film Makers*

Armes, Roy. *The Cinema of Alain Resnais.* New York: A. S. Barnes, 1968.

Barry, Iris. *D. W. Griffith: American Film Master.* New York: Museum of Modern Art, 1965.

Bogdanovich, Peter. *Allan Dwan: The Last Pioneer.* New York: Praeger, 1971.

——. *The Cinema of Alfred Hitchcock.* New York: Museum of Modern Art, 1962.

——. *The Cinema of Orson Welles.* New York: Museum of Modern Art, 1961.

——. *Fritz Lang in America.* New York: Praeger, 1969.

——. *John Ford.* Berkeley: University of California Press, 1970.

Braudy, Leo. *Jean Renoir: The World of his Films.* Garden City, N.Y.: Doubleday–Anchor, 1972.

Calder-Marshall, Arthur. *The Innocent Eye: The Life of Robert J. Flaherty.* Baltimore: Penguin, 1963.

Cameron, Ian, and Wood, Robin. *Antonioni.* New York: Praeger, 1969.

——, eds. *The Films of Jean-Luc Godard.* New York: Praeger, 1970.

——, eds. *The Films of Robert Bresson.* New York: Praeger, 1970.

Casty, Alan. *The Films of Robert Rossen.* New York: Museum of Modern Art, 1969.

Collet, Jean. *Jean-Luc Godard.* New York: Crown, 1970.

Cowie, Peter. *The Cinema of Orson Welles.* New York: A. S. Barnes, 1965.

Crisp, C. G. *François Truffaut*. New York: Praeger, 1972.

Curtiss, Thomas Quinn. *Von Stroheim*. New York: Farrar, Straus & Giroux, 1971.

Donner, Jorn. *The Personal Vision of Ingmar Bergman*. Bloomington, Ind.: Indiana University Press, 1964.

Durgnat, Raymond. *Luis Buñuel*. Berkeley: University of California Press, 1970.

Finler, Joel W. *Stroheim*. Berkeley: University of California Press, 1968.

Gibson, Arthur. *The Silence of God: Creative Response to the Films of Ingmar Bergman*. New York: Harper & Row, 1969.

Guarner, José Luis. *Roberto Rossellini*. New York: Praeger, 1970.

Higham, Charles. *The Films of Orson Welles*. Berkeley: University of California Press, 1970.

Kagan, Norman. *The Cinema of Stanley Kubrick*. New York: Holt, Rinehart and Winston, 1972.

Kyrou, Ado. *Luis Buñuel*. New York: Simon and Schuster, 1963.

Leprohon, Pierre. *Michelangelo Antonioni*. New York: Simon and Schuster, 1963.

Mussman, Toby, ed. *Jean-Luc Godard*. New York: E. P. Dutton, 1968.

Perry, George. *The Films of Alfred Hitchcock*. New York: E. P. Dutton, 1965.

Pratley, Gerald. *The Cinema of John Frankenheimer*. New York: A. S. Barnes, 1969.

Richie, Donald. *The Films of Akira Kurosawa*. Berkeley: University of California Press, 1970.

Robinson, David. *Buster Keaton*. Bloomington, Ind.: Indiana University Press, 1969.

Roud, Richard. *Godard*. Garden City, N.Y.: Doubleday, 1968.

Salachas, Gilbert. *Federico Fellini*. New York: Crown, 1969.

Solmi, Angelo. *Fellini*. New York: Humanities Press, 1967.

Steene, Brigitta. *Ingmar Bergman*. New York: Twayne, 1968.

Truffaut, François. *Hitchcock*. New York: Simon and Schuster, 1966.

Ward, John. *Alain Resnais, or The Theme of Time*. Garden City, N.Y.: Doubleday, 1968.

Weinberg, Herman G. *The Lubitsch Touch*. New York: E. P. Dutton, 1968.

Wood, Robin, and Walker, Michael. *Claude Chabrol*. New York: Praeger, 1970.

Young, Vernon. *Cinema Borealis: Ingmar Bergman and the Swedish Ethos*. New York: David Lewis, 1971.

● *Interviews with Film Makers*

Geduld, Harry M. *Film Makers on Film Making*. Bloomington, Ind.: Indiana University Press, 1967.

Gelmis, Joseph, ed. *The Film Director as Superstar*. Garden City, N.Y.: Doubleday, 1970.

Higham, Charles, and Greenberg, Joel. *The Celluloid Muse*. New York: New American Library, 1969.

Milne, Tom, ed. *Godard on Godard*. New York: Viking, 1968.

———, ed. *Losey on Losey*. Garden City, N.Y.: Doubleday, 1968.

Sarris, Andrew, ed. *Hollywood Voices*. New York: Bobbs-Merrill, 1967.

———, ed. *Interviews with Film Directors*. New York: Bobbs-Merrill, 1967.

Sherman, Eric, and Rubin, Martin. *The Director's Event: Interviews with Five American Film-Makers*. New York: Atheneum, 1970.

● *Film Scripts**

Agee, James. *Agee on Film: Five Film Scripts* (includes *The African Queen* and *The Night of the Hunter*). Boston: Beacon, 1958.

Antonioni, Michelangelo. *Screenplays of Michelangelo Antonioni: Il Grido, L'Avventura, La Notte, L'Eclisse*. New York: Orion Press, 1963.

*In addition to the excellent series of film scripts offered by Simon and Schuster, Viking Press has added a new series entitled "The MGM Library of Film Scripts," and Grossman Publishers is offering an impressive list which includes much of the early work of Antonioni, Bergman, Buñuel, Clair, Cocteau, De Sica, Eisenstein, Fellini, Rossellini, Visconti and others.

Bergman, Ingmar. *Four Screenplays of Ingmar Bergman: Smiles of a Summer Night, The Seventh Seal, Wild Strawberries, The Magician.* New York: Simon and Schuster, 1960.

————. *Three Films by Ingmar Bergman: Through A Glass Darkly, Winter Light, The Silence.* New York: Grove Press, 1967.

Buñuel, Luis. *L'Age d'Or* and *Un Chien Andalou.* New York: Simon and Schuster, 1968.

Carné, Marcel. *Children of Paradise.* New York: Simon and Schuster, 1968.

Comden, Betty, and Green, Adolph. *Singin' in the Rain.* New York: Viking, 1972.

De Sica, Vittorio. *The Bicycle Thief.* New York: Simon and Schuster, 1968.

Duras, Marguerite. *Hiroshima, Mon Amour.* New York: Grove Press, 1961.

Eisenstein, Sergei. *Potemkin.* New York: Simon and Schuster, 1968.

Fielding, Henry. *Tom Jones* (screenplay by John Osborne). New York: Grove Press, 1964.

Fellini, Federico. *Early Screenplays: Variety Lights and The White Sheik.* New York: Grossman, 1971.

————. *Fellini Satyricon.* New York: Ballantine Books, 1970.

Fonda, Peter; Hopper, Dennis; and Southern, Terry. *Easy Rider.* New York: New American Library, 1969.

Godard, Jean-Luc. *Alphaville.* New York: Simon and Schuster, 1968.

Kurosawa, Akira. *Rashomon.* New York: Grove Press, 1969.

Lehman, Ernest. *North by Northwest.* New York: Viking, 1972.

McCoy, Horace. *They Shoot Horses, Don't They?* (screenplay by Robert E. Thompson). New York: Avon, 1969.

Renoir, Jean. *Grand Illusion.* New York: Simon and Schuster, 1968.

————. *Rules of the Game.* New York: Simon and Schuster, 1970.

Robbe-Grillet, Alain. *Last Year at Marienbad.* New York: Grove Press, 1962.

Truffaut, François. *Jules and Jim.* New York: Simon and Schuster, 1968.

- *Writing for Film*

    Egri, Lajos. *The Art of Dramatic Writing*. New York: Simon and
    Schuster, 1946.

    Geduld, Harry M., ed. *Authors on Film*. Bloomington, Ind.: Indiana
    University Press, 1971.

    Parker, Norton S. *Audiovisual Script Writing*. New Brunswick, N.J.:
    Rutgers University Press, 1968.

    Roberts, Edward Barry. *Television Writing and Selling*. Cambridge,
    Mass.: Riverside Press, 1954.

    Vale, Eugene. *The Technique of Screenplay Writing*. New York:
    Grosset & Dunlap, 1972.

- *Making Films*

    Burder, John. *The Technique of Editing 16mm Films*. New York:
    Hastings House, 1968.

    Carlson, Verne, and Carlson, Sylvia. *Professional 16/35mm Camera-
    man's Handbook*. New York: AmPhoto, 1970.

    Ferguson, Robert. *How to Make Movies*. New York: Viking, 1969.

    Kuhns, William, and Giardino, Thomas F. *Behind the Camera*. Day-
    ton, Ohio: Geo. A. Pflaum, 1970.

    Lowndes, Douglas. *Film Making in Schools*. London: B. T. Batsford,
    Ltd., 1968.

    Mascelli, Joseph V., ed. *American Cinematographer Manual*. 3d ed.
    Hollywood: American Society of Cinematographers, 1969.

    ———. *The Five C's of Cinematography*. Hollywood: Cine/Grafic,
    1965.

    Pincus, Edward. *Guide to Filmmaking*. New York: New American
    Library, 1969.

    Reisz, Karel, and Millar, Gavin. *The Technique of Film Editing*. New
    York: Hastings House, 1968.

    Roberts, Kenneth H., and Sharples, Win Jr. *A Primer for Film-Making*.
    New York: Pegasus, 1971.

    Souto, H. Mario Raimondo. *The Technique of the Motion Picture
    Camera*. New York: Hastings House, 1969.

    Walter, Ernest. *The Technique of the Film Cutting Room*. New York:
    Hastings House, 1969.

- *Film and Other Arts*

Bluestone, George. *Novels into Film*. Berkeley and Los Angeles: University of California Press, 1957.

Maddux, Rachel; Silliphant, Stirling; and Isaacs, Neil D. *Fiction Into Film*. Knoxville: University of Tennessee Press, 1970.

Nicoll, Allardyce. *Film and Theatre*. New York: Crowell, 1936.

Richardson, Robert. *Literature and Film*. Bloomington: Indiana University Press.

Sheridan, Marion C., et al. *The Motion Picture and the Teaching of English*. New York: Appleton-Century-Crofts, 1965.

PERIODICALS

- *American Cinematographer*
  1728 North Orange Drive
  Hollywood, California 90028

- *Cinema Journal*
  21 Maple Avenue
  Bridgewater, Mass. 02324

- *Cinema Studies*
  1 Dane Street
  High Holborn
  London, W.C. 1, England

- *Film Comment*
  100 Walnut Place
  Brookline, Mass. 02146

- *Film Culture*
  G.P.O. Box 1499
  New York, N.Y. 10001

- *Film Heritage*
  Box 42 University of Dayton
  Dayton, Ohio 45409

- *The Film Journal*
  Box 9602
  Hollins College
  Virginia 24020

- *Films in Review*
  31 Union Square
  New York, N.Y. 10003

- *Filmmakers' Newsletter*
  P.O. Box 481
  Marblehead, N.J.

- *Film News*
  250 West 57th Street
  New York, N.Y. 10019

- *Film Quarterly*
  University of California Press
  Berkeley, California 94720

- *Film Society Review*
  144 Bleecker St.
  New York, N.Y. 10012

- *Journal of the University Film
  Association*
  156 W. 19th Avenue
  Ohio State University
  Columbus, Ohio 43210

- *Media and Methods*
  134 North 13th Street
  Philadelphia, Penn. 19107

- *New Cinema Review*
  80 Wooster Street
  New York, N.Y. 10012

- *Sight and Sound*
  British Film Institute
  81 Dean Street
  London W. 1, England

- *Screen Facts*
  Box 154
  Kew Gardens, N.Y. 11415

- *Show*
  P.O. Box 54996
  Terminal Annex
  Los Angeles, Calif. 90054

- *Super 8 Filmmaker*
  342 Madison Avenue
  New York, N.Y. 10017

- *Take One*
  Unicorn Publishers
  P.O. Box 1788 Station B
  Montreal 2, P.Q., Canada

- *Today's Film Maker*
  250 Fulton Avenue
  Hempstead, Long Island
  New York, 11550

MAJOR FILM DISTRIBUTORS FOR 16MM FILMS

- Association Films
  600 Madison Avenue
  New York, N.Y. 10022
- Audio Film Center
  (See Brandon Films)
- Avco Embassy Pictures Corporation
  1301 Avenue of the Americas
  New York, N.Y. 10019
- Brandon Films
  34 MacQuestern Parkway
  Mount Vernon, N.Y. 10550
- Budget Films
  4590 Santa Monica Boulevard
  Los Angeles, Calif. 90029
- Canyon Cinema Cooperative
  756 Union Street
  San Francisco, Calif. 94101
- Cinema 16/Grove Press
  80 University Place
  New York, N.Y. 10003
- Columbia Cinematheque
  711 Fifth Avenue
  New York, N.Y. 10022
- Contemporary Films/McGraw-Hill
  330 W. 42nd Street
  New York, N.Y.
    Midwest:
  828 Custer Avenue
  Evanston, Illinois 60202
    West
  1714 Stockton Street
  San Francisco, Calif. 94133
- Continental 16, Inc.
  241 East 34th Street
  New York, N.Y. 10016
- Creative Film Society
  14558 Valerio Street
  Van Nuys, Calif. 91405

- Cultural Films
  1564 Broadway
  New York, N.Y. 10036
- Don Bosco Films
  148 Main Street
  New Rochelle, N.Y. 10802
- Encyclopaedia Britannica
  Education Corporation
  425 North Michigan Ave.
  Chicago, Illinois 60611
- Em Gee Film Library
  Glenn Photo Supply
  4931 Gloria Avenue
  Encino, Calif. 91316
- Entertainment Films
  850 Seventh Avenue
  New York, N.Y. 10019
- Factory Films, Inc.
  33 Union Square West
  New York, N.Y. 10003
- Film Classic Exchange
  1926 S. Vermont Avenue
  Los Angeles, Calif. 90007
- Film Images
  17 West 60th Street
  New York, N.Y. 10023
- Film-makers Cooperative
  175 Lexington Avenue
  New York, N.Y. 10016
- Films Incorporated
  4420 Oakton Street
  Skokie, Illinois 60076
    and
  1150 Wilmette Avenue
  Wilmette, Illinois 60091
- Ideal Pictures
  1010 Church Street
  Evanston, Illinois 60201

- Indiana University
  Audio-Visual Center
  Bloomington, Indiana 47401
- Institutional Cinema Service
  20 East 10th Street
  New York, N.Y. 10003
  Midwest:
  203 North Wabash Avenue
  Chicago, Illinois 60601
  West:
  2323 Van Ness Avenue
  San Francisco, Calif. 94109
- International Film Bureau Inc.
  332 South Michigan Avenue
  Chicago, Illinois 60604
- Janus Film Library
  24 West 58th Street
  New York, N.Y. 10019
- Leacock-Pennebaker
  56 W. 45th Street
  New York, N.Y. 10036
- Learning Corporation of America
  711 Fifth Avenue
  New York, N.Y. 10022
- Movie Classics
  P.O. Box 1463
  Philadelphia, Penn. 19105
- Museum of Modern Art
  Department of Film—Film Library
  11 West 53rd Street
  New York, N.Y. 10019
- National Film Board of Canada
  680 Fifth Avenue, Suite 819
  New York, N.Y. 10019
- New Line Cinema
  121 University Place
  New York, N.Y. 10003
- New Yorker Films
  2409 Broadway
  New York, N.Y. 10024

- Pyramid Films
  Box 1048
  Santa Monica, Calif. 90406
- Radim Films
  220 West 42nd Street
  New York, N.Y. 10036
- Rembrandt Film Library
  267 West 25th Street
  New York, N.Y. 10001
- Roa's Films
  1696 North Astor St.
  Milwaukee, Wisconsin 53202
- Standard Film Service
  14710 W. Warren Avenue
  Dearborn, Michigan 48120
  and
  21702 Grand River
  Detroit, Michigan 48219
- Trans-National Films
  332 S. Michigan Avenue
  Chicago, Illinois 60604
- United Artists 16
  729 Seventh Avenue
  New York, N.Y. 10019
- United World Films
  221 Park Avenue South
  New York, N.Y. 10003
  Midwest:
  542 South Dearborn
  Chicago, Illinois 60605
  West:
  1025 North Highland Avenue
  Los Angeles, Calif. 90038
- Universal Kinetic
  221 Park Avenue South
  New York, N.Y. 10003
- Warner Brothers, Inc.
  Non-theatrical Division
  666 Fifth Avenue
  New York, N.Y. 10019

Index

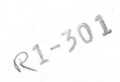